# CAMBRIDGE LIBRA

Books of enduring s

## Cambridge

The city of Cambridge received its royal charter in 1201, having already been home to Britons, Romans and Anglo-Saxons for many centuries. Cambridge University was founded soon afterwards and celebrates its octocentenary in 2009. This series explores the history and influence of Cambridge as a centre of science, learning, and discovery, its contributions to national and global politics and culture, and its inevitable controversies and scandals.

## By-Ways of Cambridge History

As an early student at Newnham College and subsequently as the wife of John Neville Keynes, Florence Ada Keynes (née Brown, (1861–1958) spent her entire adult life living in Cambridge. A prominent public figure, active in charity work and public service, she became the first female councillor of the city and served as its Mayor in 1932. This charming little book was published when she was 86 years old. It displays her wide knowledge and love of the city of Cambridge, with engaging essays on Barnwell Priory, the history of the old Market Cross and Conduit and of town planning and social housing in Cambridge. Keynes tells of famous personalities from the city's past, such as the seventeenth-century philosopher Damaris Cudworth and the composer Orlando Gibbons, and recounts more personal memories of the changes her generation lived through, making this a valuable record of her own life.

Cambridge University Press has long been a pioneer in the reissuing of out-of-print titles from its own backlist, producing digital reprints of books that are still sought after by scholars and students but could not be reprinted economically using traditional technology. The Cambridge Library Collection extends this activity to a wider range of books which are still of importance to researchers and professionals, either for the source material they contain, or as landmarks in the history of their academic discipline.

Drawing from the world-renowned collections in the Cambridge University Library, and guided by the advice of experts in each subject area, Cambridge University Press is using state-of-the-art scanning machines in its own Printing House to capture the content of each book selected for inclusion. The files are processed to give a consistently clear, crisp image, and the books finished to the high quality standard for which the Press is recognised around the world. The latest print-on-demand technology ensures that the books will remain available indefinitely, and that orders for single or multiple copies can quickly be supplied.

The Cambridge Library Collection will bring back to life books of enduring scholarly value across a wide range of disciplines in the humanities and social sciences and in science and technology.

# By-Ways of
# Cambridge History

FLORENCE ADA KEYNES

CAMBRIDGE
UNIVERSITY PRESS

CAMBRIDGE UNIVERSITY PRESS

Cambridge New York Melbourne Madrid Cape Town Singapore São Paolo Delhi

Published in the United States of America by Cambridge University Press, New York

www.cambridge.org
Information on this title: www.cambridge.org/9781108002332

This edition first published 1947
This digitally printed version 2009

ISBN 978-1-108-00233-2

BY-WAYS OF
CAMBRIDGE
HISTORY

*Remnants of history which have casually
escaped the shipwreck of Time.*

FRANCIS BACON: *The Advancement of Learning*

Plate I. Petty Cury, by J. M. Ince, 1838
Published in *Cambridge Portfolio*, 1840

# BY-WAYS OF
# CAMBRIDGE
# HISTORY

By
F. A. KEYNES

CAMBRIDGE
At the University Press
1947

Printed in Great Britain at the University Press, Cambridge
(Brooke Crutchley, University Printer)
and published by the Cambridge University Press
(Cambridge, and Bentley House, London)
Agents for U.S.A., Canada, and India: Macmillan

# PREFACE

IT has not been possible to mention in the text or the footnotes all the references to the Charters edited by Professor Maitland and Miss Mary Bateson; to the Annals compiled by Mr C. H. Cooper, formerly Town Clerk; to the works of Mr J. W. Clark (including the Clark collection of papers in the University Library); and to the valuable publications of the Cambridge Antiquarian Society. Access to the Minutes of the Cambridge Improved Industrial Dwellings Co. (Chap. VIII) was obtained by the courtesy of the late Mr A. B. Chater, Secretary to the Company, and permission to incorporate (Chap. III) an article on the 'Origin and Early Years of Orlando Gibbons', which appeared in the *Monthly Musical Record*, October 1936, has been kindly granted by Messrs Augener Ltd.

I am further indebted to many friends for assistance in various ways. Special thanks are due to Mr J. H. Bullock, a life-long student of Cambridge history and topography, to Dr Helen Cam, and to the Town Clerks of the Boroughs mentioned.

F. A. KEYNES

# CONTENTS

# ILLUSTRATIONS

# Illustrations

# INTRODUCTORY

IT is rash for an amateur to venture upon a field of inquiry long and thoroughly worked by experts. The only excuse I can offer for presuming to write on a quasi-historical subject, lies in the hope that I may succeed in interesting some of those who share my love of Cambridge and desire to know more of her past without having the time or the opportunity to consult authorities for themselves.

My own interest is of long-standing. I came to live in Cambridge on my marriage sixty-four years ago, having been before that time one of the early students at Newnham, then a Hall of residence with rooms for about thirty. Those early students, many of them of mature age, pursued their studies under the more than maternal eye of Miss Anne Jemima Clough. Their kind friends in Cambridge, with Henry Sidgwick as leader, who were deeply interested in providing opportunities for women to obtain University education, were naturally anxious as to the impression they would make in a community where there were many critics. If the movement was to succeed, it must be very cautiously introduced and carefully guided. The task was not an easy one, but if the more emancipated spirits were sometimes irked by restrictions which seemed tiresome and unnecessary, the situation was in the main accepted cheerfully, and it was recognized that the advantages far outweighed the disabilities.

The desire of our Principal, Miss Clough, to whom we owed so much, was that we should be as inconspicuous as possible not only in behaviour but also in appearance, in order not to alarm the doubters—and here some difference of opinion arose. A period of dreary dowdiness in clothing and house decoration had persisted through the seventies, but towards the end of the decade reaction came in a riot of colour, 'when the shining morning of the Pre-Raphael Brotherhood dawned upon middle-class comfort'. Rossetti was painting women—or one woman, his wife—with burnished red-gold hair, clothed in purple and blue. Burne-Jones drew willowy forms clad in rainbow hues, William Morris wove textiles rampant in design;[1] dyers dipped silk and wool in all the Pre-Raphaelite tinctures. Newnham caught the fever. We trailed about in clinging robes of peacock blue, terra-cotta red, sage green or orange, feeling very brave and thoroughly enjoying the sensation it caused. Poor Miss Clough! Her students were the observed of all observers.

Fortunately, the fine efforts of the educationalists did not end in fiasco. Newnham calmed down and the good sound work done in the budding college bore fruit.

The pioneers into whose company I was admitted included outstanding personalities: Jane Harrison, the Greek

[1] When I married I clothed my house in Morris wall-paper, which still remains in my dining-room in very decent condition.

Interest in the Pre-Raphaelites seems to be reviving. The Poet Laureate has published an elaborate analysis of some of Rossetti's poems; a learned American interpretation of *William Morris, Medievalist and Revolutionary* has appeared, of which a reviewer says: 'The ghost of William Morris may feel a little uneasy in that new and highly industrialised country, but he will awake one day to find himself all the rage, the saint of a new aesthetic religion, with robes and stained glass windows already designed.' *Observer*, 19 May 1946.

Plate II. Miss Clough and the writer, 1880

Plate III. Return from the May Races

(*See* p. xx)

scholar; Penelope Lawrence, founder of Roedean School; Helen Gladstone, later a Vice-Principal; Margaret Merrifield, a College lecturer, long known in Cambridge as the wife and helper of Dr Verrall; Mary Martin, full of Irish wit and enthusiasm, who became the wife of the philosopher, James Ward; Alice Werner, the expert in African languages, of whom it used to be said that she alone of Europeans could produce the authentic 'click'; and many others who in their subsequent careers paved the way for further advances in the higher education and professional advancement of women. They builded better than they knew, and their dreams certainly did not include a vision of Newnham providing Professors for the University— although still standing outside full membership of that body.

It was the age of chaperones. Miss Helen Gladstone had a special joke that I, being the youngest of the students, should be the official chaperone. Miss Clough, however, did not regard me in that light, and I, having gone inadvertently with a family friend to her brother's rooms in College, was in deep disgrace. Somehow such lapses never failed to come to our Principal's ears. The chaperone system survived in full strength in the women's colleges for a long period, as it did indeed in general society. I remember hearing how my husband, then a young lecturer, went to coach at Girton in the middle seventies, and was taken aback to find the Mistress of the College, complete with knitting needles, installed in the room to watch over his staid pupil, senior to himself, and who eventually became Mistress of the College.

An important stage for women students in Cambridge

was reached in 1881, and great was the excitement when a Grace was passed, by 398 votes to 32, admitting women to Tripos examinations formally, as of right, instead of by favour of the examiners. A Newnham student wrote a lively description of the event to her family, telling how Miss Helen Gladstone, then in residence, telegraphed to her father and got a special train put on, so that members of parliament could come to vote and return in time for an important division in the House of Commons; how the Senate House was so crowded that since the vote had to be given sitting, Masters of Arts queued up for seats; how the good news of victory was signalled by flags and handkerchiefs to a student on horseback waiting at the Backs. The writer ended with the words: 'When women get degrees, it will be nothing to this, we all feel it is the great crisis in the history of women's Colleges.'

In 1882 I joined the ranks of residents in the town; it was at a moment when University society was suddenly transformed by the new Statutes which gave general permission to Fellows of Colleges to retain their Fellowships after marriage.

This great change was the end of a long controversy which can perhaps be traced back to the question of the celibacy of the clergy. Queen Elizabeth disliked the freedom given them for marriage at the Reformation, and in 1559 decreed that no Head of a College should marry without the approval of the Visitor of the College, normally a Bishop, and that no priest or deacon should marry unless his future wife had been approved by the Bishop of the Diocese and two Justices of the same shire.

In 1776 there was an ineffectual attempt to obtain a

Grace of the Senate for appointing a syndicate to petition
Parliament that Fellows should not lose their Fellowships
on marriage. The Rev. William Cole, in his account of the
proceedings, says:

> There were those who would not believe it was or could
> be intended in earnest; who imagined it must be a jest only.
> However, the projectors and abettors of the scheme were in
> earnest. Accordingly a Grace was drawn up and brought into
> the House.

The original mover withdrew and 'there was the greatest
confusion imaginable, but this excited and heightened the
warmth and ardour of the partisans. Nothing was determined at the Congregation. But', Cole adds, 'the party
continues hot, and is in hopes of downing to the ground
with Celibacy.' After another vain attempt in 1798 there
was in the course of last century some slight relaxation of
the rule of celibacy in two or three of the colleges in
varying degree, but nothing comprehensive until the
Statutes of 1882. This change, which came just too late to
allow my husband to keep his Fellowship at Pembroke,
was inevitable if Cambridge was to attract and keep the
services of scientists, who were required in increasing
numbers, and who had no such resource as the earlier
type of don, usually in holy orders, who could take a
college living if he wished to marry; it was part of the
general adaptation of the University to modern conditions.
Thus Cambridge became a place where women could
be educated and men could be married, and the results
have not seldom been combined. Many children were
brought up together in the first generation of University

offspring, a small fresh society where we all knew one another.

Social life still had much of the formality typical of Victorian days, especially emphasized perhaps in University circles where order of precedence was a ruling feature. Before the influx of new life in 1882, few had been admitted into the inner circle beyond Heads of Houses and Professors with their ladies. The young brides were, however, received hospitably and formal dinner parties were graced by them one at a time in turn, sometimes to their embarrassment. Etiquette demanded that the bride should appear in her bridal gown and be taken in to dinner by the host. For this occasion only, she was the leading lady; she had to be on the alert to catch the hostess's eye when the suitable moment came for the ladies to withdraw, and hers it was to rise and precede the train of stately dowagers into the withdrawing-room.

When it became her duty to return this hospitality, it was a real puzzle not only to provide the seven or eight courses of the dinner but also to arrange the guests at table in proper order. The husband usually had to solve the problem by explaining exactly how the expected guests would walk in an official procession.

For the children of the house, when they were old enough to escape from the night nursery and lie in ambush on the stairs, it was all great fun. The waiters, a kindly set of men with children of their own, willingly paid toll and the melting ice-bomb speedily disappeared.

What did Cambridge look like then? Approach was by rail; there was little or no road-travel, which then seemed to be a thing of the past, not of the future. First impressions were therefore given by the Station which had been opened in 1845, and in a publication of that date was described as follows:

The entire structure is extremely chaste and elegant in its proportions and remarkable for the convenience of its arrangements. The details are characterised by bold cornices and mouldings, and by an extreme simplicity of ornamental enrichment.

A description at the present time would probably be less eulogistic.

The distance from this impressive structure to the centre of the Town was covered by a one-horse tram. It was a slow journey, and if undertaken now in the same way would give time for noticing the changes. The famous landmark of the Roman Catholic Church built by Mrs Lyne Stephens was not yet there, the site given by the fifteenth Duke of Norfolk being occupied by a house surrounded by a brick wall overhung with lilac bushes. A magnificent poplar, which long survived in a mutilated form, was then in its glory at the corner of Lensfield Road. On the other side of the Hills Road there was no Perse School; it was then in Free School Lane.

In St Andrew's Street there was no imposing Police Station. On part of its present site there was Hobson's Spinning House, where disorderly women were taken by the proctors and detained—a system which continued until 1894. Next came the Baptist Chapel, then a plain oblong building standing back from the road, with no windows to the front, a precaution said to have been taken from fear that they might be the subject of attack by undergraduates.

In the Cury there were still some finely decorated houses, and Falcon Yard was surrounded by the wooden galleries and stairs that had survived with little change for centuries.

Downing Street must be imagined as denuded of its scientific buildings, with the exception of the Natural History Museum on the old site of the Physic Garden, and with the iron gates of the garden still standing. Those gates now form the Trumpington Road entrance to the Botanic Garden. On the other side of Downing Street, there was an open view through Downing College grounds to Lensfield Road.

Harvey Road, which is still our home, was named, in the praiseworthy Cambridge fashion of commemorating great men, after William Harvey, whom our children firmly believed to have devised the circulation of the blood. My impression is that when I first saw the road, before our house was built, it was a private road, with iron gates across the entrance. The land then was, and still is, the property of Caius College, part of the territory marked off as belonging to the College by the award of 1807 when the open fields of Barnwell,[1] in which the College had a share, were enclosed. One of the allotments made to the College under this scheme consisted roughly of the land now bounded by Gonville Place, Hills Road, St Paul's Road, and Gresham Road, and since the original holding had come to the College from the Mortimers of Newnham and Attleborough, their property was still known as Mortimer's Dole, or share.

[1] See also 'Barnwell Priory', Ch. IV, p. 106.

( xviii )

## Introductory

The houses, which were built in Harvey Road about 1882, and did something towards meeting the needs of the newly married dons, were still very much in the 'open fields'. My children looked from their nursery window across 'Bulman's field', where the drovers kept their cattle over the week-end, ready for the Monday market, and the lowing of the cows was a familiar sound. With the exception of the houses in Station Road there was, indeed, little or nothing between us and the Gogs. Roads were of the old macadamized sort, and after wet weather great pools of liquid mud were swept to the sides of the road, while in dry weather the dust was intolerable, despite an occasional sprinkling by a water-cart.

Cambridge was not only without motor vehicles, but practically without bicycles. The only type then in use was the old high machine, rarely seen in the town, with a front wheel sometimes measuring five feet in height.[1] 'Safety' bicycles, invented in 1876, were first marketed in practicable form in 1885; pneumatic tyres were not attained until 1889, and free-wheels in 1894.

In the eighties and nineties, May week visitors made more mark than now, and the May Races created a more general flutter. Going down to Ditton in a car or on bicycles is a far less important event than making up a party, engaging a suitable rowing-boat, securing stalwart undergraduates to row, packing tea-apparatus, and making an early start to the boating sheds in a horse-drawn carriage, in order to obtain a good place at Ditton Corner.

[1] The bicycle in its first form was invented in 1839 by Kirkpatrick Macmillan, a Scots blacksmith, known as 'The Devil on Wheels'. It has been estimated that at least seventy million bicycles are now in use.

The return journey was equally thrilling—the river solid with boats, the scramble to get out first from the moorings, the risk of having the rudder removed, the splashing of the Cam water over summer gowns, pushing off other boats and scoring off them, avoiding the returning 'eights', and the triumph of landing in time to get to a College Concert or Supper-party.

Large barges with a covered saloon in the centre providing elevated seats on the top were popular for large parties. These were horse-drawn, and when the rope sagged—at Barnwell Pool, for instance—children were in peril of being caught and dragged into the Cam, as sometimes actually happened.

The river was crossed here and there by a 'grind', a wooden platform drawn by an iron chain, which with much jerking and groaning was worked from the bank by a hand-crank—in one instance by a horse. At the end of a race there would be a rush of spectators from the tow-path to the meadows, and I remember an occasion when a serious-minded individual wishing to cross in the opposite direction was repeatedly thwarted by the crowd when he tried to land and driven back to the other side.

The most rapid means of conveyance was by hansom cab, a lightly built cabriolet for two passengers. The driver sat on a high perch behind the cab, with the reins passing over the top; the only way of communicating with him was by pushing open a small trap-door in the roof. The horse used in a hansom was usually a throw-out from Newmarket, sometimes one past racing, sometimes a comparative youngster who had not realized the owner's hopes. In either case the pace was prodigious and could not quickly be checked by the driver. This was a serious danger when these cabs came racing recklessly along Hills Road to the Station.

The recreations and excitements of last century may seem tame to the present generation, but the young people had their thrills, though they knew nothing of pace as it is reckoned now, and nothing of many other things—good and bad—that are commonplaces to-day. We could say even then—like two old Cambridgeshire countrymen, whose talk I overheard in a train—'Lots of things have come about since we've been about.'

From my earliest days in Cambridge, I felt the spell that the Town casts over so many of her citizens, and by the time my children passed out of the nursery stage, I was ready to take a share in work for the community. The following chapters, with few exceptions, took form during the long period when I was in close contact with local activities; the subjects, though appearing detached, meet at various points and even occasionally overlap, while emphasizing one aspect or another of the Cambridge background.

The chapter on Mendicity House (Chap. viii) might have been used as an introduction, since it was drawn up for the Cambridge Central Aid Society (formerly the Charity Organization Society, inaugurated in Cambridge by Dr Henry Sidgwick), to which I owed an intimate acquaintance with the borough dating from the early nineties. This knowledge of local conditions provided a basis for many years of work with the Poor Law from 1907, when a seat on the Board of Guardians was regarded as hardly suitable for a woman, until its transformation into Public Assistance in 1930—having taken my turn as Chairman of the Board.

My membership of the Borough Council began in August 1914, when an Act of Parliament made it possible for married women to become candidates for seats on County and Borough Councils. The position had previously been strangely anomalous, since married women could not be councillors or aldermen of a county council (other than that of London) or of a municipal borough council (except a metropolitan borough), whereas unmarried women could be. The change was brought about by placing qualification of candidates upon twelve months' residence for men and women alike, instead of restricting it to householders. In the eye of the law, no married woman could qualify as a householder, with the result that only a comparatively small number of spinsters and widows had been eligible.

Further barriers were removed at the end of the War of 1914–18, with the admission of women to legal appointments, and Cambridge took the lead with a larger number of women magistrates than any other borough in the first list in 1920. My interest in the work of the bench was increased by chairmanship for many years of a committee in London of the National Council of Women of Great Britain—a committee which was attended by women magistrates from all parts of the country.

The claims of Cambridge as my main interest were, however, never weakened, and with 1932—our Golden Wedding year—came election to the Mayoralty of the Borough. During my Mayoral year there happened to be an unusually large number of national and international conferences meeting in Cambridge. We had, for instance, the pleasure of receiving the Royal Institute of British Architects with Sir Raymond Unwin as President, the first visit of the Institute to Cambridge, followed by the conference of the Transport and General Workers' Union, when Mr Ernest Bevin was present as General Secretary. There were many others.

It was in connexion with one of the international conferences, the International Society for Musical Research, of which Professor E. J. Dent was President, that my attention was first directed to Orlando Gibbons. I was about to claim him—in an address to the Conference—as a native of Cambridge, when I was warned that this was a controversial subject.

A few weeks later it was my privilege as Mayor to accompany to Oxford those members of the Corporation, who were enthusiastic players of the historic game of bowls, to meet like-minded enthusiasts from Oxford City Council in an annual competition. It was a blazing afternoon in August, and after having made a deplorably bad opening for my side on the bowling green, I took refuge in a cooler interlude of research. Then it was that I saw the entry of the baptism of Orlando Gybbins (*sic*) on Christmas Day 1583, marked with a small cross in red ink. It would be interesting to know if the mark was placed there by Anthony Wood, the first to notice it. When I found time to investigate the question further, some of my results were published in an article in the *Monthly Musical Record* for October 1936. To this has now been added a general survey of Cambridge Waits (Ch. III).

Damaris Cudworth (Ch. VI) was brought to my notice

## By-ways of Cambridge History

by Mrs Graham Wallas, in her book *Before the Blue-stockings*, and it seemed worth while to collect more information about this outstanding Cambridge woman. Part of this chapter was published in the local *Public Library Record* in December 1932.

Town and Country planning was frequently under discussion, and in *The Times* notice in 1936 of the bi-centenary of Hawksmoor's death there was a reference to his Town Plan for Cambridge (Ch. vii) that led to a search in the British Museum. Quite recently, through the courtesy of the Keeper of the Map Room and the Librarian of the National Library of Wales, a photograph of the plan has been obtained, the original having been placed in safe custody at Aberystwyth during the war.

At the termination of my year as Mayor, the chairmanship of the committee charged with carrying out the decisions of the Council for building a new Guildhall fell to me, and it was in the course of this lengthy undertaking that the history of the Guildhall and Market Place (Ch. I) emerged as an agreeable diversion.

With increased leisure, after retiring from many public engagements just before the outbreak of the War of 1939–45, I found great pleasure in the development of the Cambridge and County Folk Museum. My special interest in Barnwell Priory (Ch. iv) naturally followed when the remaining available portion of the site of the Priory, together with the Old Abbey House, was presented by Lord Fairhaven to the Association, of which he was President, for the future home of an enlarged Folk Museum.

The inquiry into the history of the Office of High

Plate IV.  The last hansom cab in Cambridge

(*See* p. xx)

Plate V. Cambridge Market Place, 1820

Showing some of the houses demolished in 1849. From an original water-colour drawing by J. S. Cotman. (*See* p. 5)

Steward of the Borough of Cambridge (Ch. II) appeared first in 1944 as a separate brochure, but has now received considerable additions. The one digression from the history of the borough into the almost forgotten rivalries between the two Universities of Oxford and Cambridge in 'Why Oxford comes First' (Ch. v) may perhaps be forgiven in view of my husband's continuous connexion with the latter since the year 1872. As Registry Emeritus he is now keeping his two hundred and twenty-third term by residence.

Much of this sounds sadly egotistical, but reminiscences are difficult to keep impersonal, and this slight sketch may be taken as applying to the work of women in general, indicating in barest outline the early days of the great change that has been taking place during the last half century in the opportunities for women to contribute their share in work for the community—work which has borne such rich fruit during the War of 1939–45, when the writer of these pages has been merely an onlooker.

FLORENCE ADA KEYNES

6 *Harvey Road*
*Cambridge*

*May* 1946

# CHAPTER I

# THE GUILDHALL & THE MARKET PLACE

CAMBRIDGE has sometimes been described as being built like Rome on Seven Hills, but, if the theory of its dual origin is accepted, a theory for which there is much weight of expert opinion, another description may be suggested. Starting from the supposition that Mercians and East Anglians occupied sites separated only by a stream slightly to the north of the course of the river as it now flows under Magdalene Bridge, we get the interesting juxtaposition of two towns each built on its own hills in close proximity, but with little intercourse, since they were inhabited by hostile nationalities. As Arthur Gray said, the impact of the nationalities was at Cambridge.

The relative antiquity of the two settlements is uncertain, but that which was certainly the more important commercially, was centred on its four hills—Senate House Hill, Market Hill, Peas Hill, St Andrew's Hill—hillocks rather than hills,[1] standing slightly above the surrounding marshy ground, levelled out of recognition now by the hand of time helped by the hand of man. Arthur Gray, writing in 1908, said:

For four centuries and longer Cambridge has been steadily

---

[1] When excavations were being made for the Arts Theatre, it was found that the summit of Peas Hill was somewhere about where the stalls at the back now stand. Since the dressing-rooms below the stage are at about sea-level, the height of the 'hill' is well indicated.

raising the level of the grounds on the western side of the river. We have seen the process going on in recent years on Queens' Green and in Trinity Paddocks. It was going on in 1475, when the town covenanted with Queens' College to be allowed to deposit rubbish on the space between the College grove and the road leading to Newnham.[1]

Gray goes on to quote Bowtell as saying in 1805:

The grounds on the back of the Colleges, lying on the west side of the river, have been considerably raised within the last 20 years, especially in 1791-2-3, by means of earth taken out of the churchyards of St. Michael, St. Edward, Great St. Mary, All Saints [then in Trinity Street], Great St. Andrew, St. Giles and St. Sepulchre.

The other town, although smaller, stood proudly upon its higher ground culminating in three hills—now called Castle Hill, Honey Hill and Pound Hill (Mount Pleasant, being merely the side of Castle Hill). It may be a remnant of the almost forgotten tradition of a separate fortified city or *burh* that led the men of Castle End in quite recent times to refer to themselves habitually as the 'Borough Boys'. But if the Mercians, as the keepers of the Castle and Bridge, were masters of the military position, the more civilized East Anglians held the trading centres. 'The market, the mills, the three Cambridge fairs [Sturbridge Fair, Midsummer Fair, Garlic Fair] all belonged to the southern town.'[2]

The amalgamation of the two centres probably took place very gradually over a long period, as the result of pressure from Danish invasion in the ninth century and of

[1] Arthur Gray, *The Dual Origin of the Town of Cambridge*, p. 19.
[2] Gray, *op. cit.* p. 13.

later political and economic changes, but there can be no doubt that for the last seven centuries the corporate life of the whole town has been firmly rooted in the plot of ground south of Market Hill.

The first building there put to public use was a house already standing, the house of Benjamin the Jew, of which possession was granted to the town by Henry III in 1224 for a gaol. The story begins, therefore, with the enforcement of law and order.

It is interesting to note that a house belonging to Moses, the son of Isaac, was similarly given to the citizens of Oxford by Henry III in 1229. This house, which is supposed to have come to the King by escheat, occupied part of the site of the present municipal buildings, as in Cambridge. It was used as the Guildhall, and next to it Henry himself established a *Domus Conversorum*, or home for converted Jews.[1]

The establishment of the Jews in England was one of the incidental effects of the Conquest. They had followed in the wake of the invading army, finding ready money for the impoverished English, and generally meeting a universally felt need for money-broking of all kinds. They had a free field for such activities, for the idea that advantage must not be taken of the necessities of one's kindred had been adopted in Europe by the Church, and in England it was unlawful at common law for a Christian to take interest on money lent, a prohibition enforced by various medieval enactments on usury.[2]

[1] C. W. Boase, *Oxford*, pp. 23, 24, in series of 'Historic Towns'.
[2] Bellot, 'Money-Lending' in *Encyclopaedia Britannica*, 14th ed. p. 699.

1-2

This feeling persisted for a long time. Sir Simonds D'Ewes, in his *Autobiography*, in 1633 said:

> My credit would have suffered [sufficed, late M.E.] to have borrowed many thousands in London, had I needed it; but my scruple that I thought it not lawful to give or take use [usury] made the difficulty that I could not borrow in the ordinary way.

How it was that the house of Benjamin the Jew became vacant is not recorded. It may have fallen in to the Crown, as in Oxford. By that time, however, the wealth and consequent power of the Jews was decreasing, and they were expelled from Cambridge in 1275. Until that date, they seem to have been allowed to remain in the area between the old All Saints' Church opposite St John's College and the Round Church in Bridge Street, long known as the Old Jewry. The action of Edward I, who in 1290 expelled the Jews from the country, compelled his subjects to undertake their own financial life unaided by Jewry, so that when in Cromwell's time the Jews were allowed to return, the English had learnt to stand alone.[1]

The old Synagogue which adjoined Benjamin's house was assigned by the Bailiffs of Cambridge to the Franciscan or Grey Friars, until about fifty years later they found a more commodious home by building an imposing Convent which they occupied for about three centuries where Sidney Sussex now stands. The building they had vacated was then adapted as a Town Hall, or Tolbooth as it was commonly called, its chief business being the collection of market tolls.

[1] Trevelyan, *English Social History*, p. 82.

## The Guildhall & the Market Place

In 1374 this hall having fallen into decay was replaced by another on the same site. Again it was on simple lines, providing little more than a room for meetings, and being raised on arches it formed a shelter for the market below. The walls of the hall were covered with hangings and the floor was strewn with rushes; in addition to being used for public purposes, it was let to private persons for marriage feasts, known as 'brydales'. This primitive building was not demolished until 1782, having then served the Town for four hundred years. All this time the gaol stood beside it, part being portioned off for witches as late as the middle of the seventeenth century. In 1645 a woman was hanged in Cambridge for witchcraft. The Witchcraft and Vagrancy Act abolishing prosecution for witchcraft by making it illegal to *pretend* to the powers of witchcraft was not passed until as late as 1736; within the last fifty years fortune-tellers have been prosecuted under that Act.

The space left free for the general market was much congested. There was a large block of houses and shops on the west side, at the back of Great St Mary's Church, and near the front of the Guildhall stood a conduit, erected in 1614, known as Hobson's Conduit.[1] It was not until 1855, after a serious fire in 1849, that the west side was cleared of buildings—a great enterprise—and the conduit was then removed to the corner of the Town end of Trumpington Road, and replaced by another in the centre of the enlarged Market Place.

[1] Thomas Hobson left money in his Will for enlarging the conduit, but the money for the original erection was not provided entirely by him.

Slightly to the west of the original conduit, and on the south-west corner of the Market, was a Cross of unknown date, standing on what was called Green Hill, the Herb Market, where garden-stuff was sold. Near the Cross were the stocks for the correction of evil-doers, and the pillory was placed there when required. The Cross was raised on a platform reached by several stone steps and was protected by a circular lead-covered roof supported on four wooden pillars. No satisfactory drawing of it is known, but the best outline is contained in a plan by Braun, published in Cologne in 1575. Although this is not reliable as a plan of the Town, it happens that the old Market Cross is given in slightly more detail than in any other map.[1]

The Cross served many public purposes, and the whole erection with its steps, pillars and canopy must have been of considerable size as it was the setting for many celebrations. In 1529, in the reign of Henry VIII, when the Mayor was excommunicated by the Vice-Chancellor for refusing to answer a charge of having violated the privileges of the University, the document of excommunication was affixed to the Market Cross.[2] This use of the Cross, or more probably the pillars of the Cross, seems to have been a common practice, for in 1546 there was a charge in the Treasurers' accounts for 'small nayles to nayle on the proclamacions on the market crosse'. Sometimes the 'small nayles' seem to have been used for more

[1] See p. 20.
[2] The Mayor had to do penance in the Church of the Friars Augustine, 'holding a candle, the price of a half-penny in his hand, and kneeling on his knees openly before the image of our Lady', and afterwards signing a written submission before the excommunication was withdrawn.

unpleasant purposes. Lord North, when Lord Lieutenant in 1569—soon afterwards to be High Steward of the Borough—was a strenuous defender of the liberties of the Town in its contentions with the University, and there is a letter of his addressed to the Vice-Chancellor in which he refers to the conduct of some student who had used 'evyll and fowle wordes' to the Mayor. He adjudges 'the varlet' to stand in the pillory for three hours with one ear nailed to the same, and to ask the forgiveness of the Mayor on his knees; afterwards, to pleasure the University, he remitted the ear-nailing, 'so as he stand 3 howers on the Pillorye'.[1]

The Market Cross appears frequently throughout the Borough records. In 1553 the Duke of Northumberland, High Steward of the Borough,[2] who had persuaded Edward VI to settle the Crown on the Lady Jane Grey, arrived in Cambridge with a large force, in her support. Her rival, Mary Tudor, was then at Framlingham Castle in Suffolk. When the Duke found his forces deserting him and reinforcements failing to arrive, 'he came to the market crosse of the towne and calling for an Herault, himself proclaimed queene Mary, and among other he threwe up his own cappe'.[3] On this occasion he 'so laughed that the tears ran down his face for grief'. He hoped in vain to save his life; that evening he was taken from Cambridge to the Tower of London and ten days later he was beheaded there. At a more cheerful time,

[1] MSS. Baker, xxix, 398, and Arthur Gray, *Town of Cambridge*, p. 102.
[2] See also 'High Stewards', Ch. II, p. 38.
[3] Stow, *Annales*, ed. 1605, p. 1033.

when preparations were being made for Elizabeth's visit in 1564, considerable payments were made for painting the Cross and mending the lead. In 1593 almost 2200 lb. of lead was taken from the Cross and sold; the large quantity indicates that this was the time when the canopy was removed. At the Restoration, the proclamation of Charles II took place there, and also at the centre of the Market Place.

A few years later, in 1664, the old Cross disappeared and was replaced by one totally different, described in a Cambridge Guide, published in 1763, as a 'handsome square stone pillar of the Ionick Order; on the top of which is an Orb and cross gilt'.[1] From the steps of this new erection, James II was proclaimed, the Vice-Chancellor and Senior Bedell standing upon the steps, which may have been the original base of the old Cross. George III also was proclaimed there, with a procession on horse-back and music. In 1740, when a serious riot took place between the scholars and the Town, a proclamation to restrain the rioters was read from the Market Cross.

In 1786, after the second Cross had stood there for over a hundred years, having been repaired at considerable cost in 1754, the Corporation 'ordered that the Market Cross be removed to some more convenient place', and appointed a committee 'to consider of a more proper place, if they think a cross necessary'. William Cole, the antiquary, had protested in 1779 that the Cross was being neglected. He complains in his *Diary* of the people who have suffered 'the beautiful gilded cross on the Market Hill at Cambridge to be defaced, and the magistrates for

[1] *Cantabrigia Depicta*, p. 10.

( 8 )

these 10 years or more have never had spirit enough to repair it. I mentioned it', he writes, 'this year to Mr John Forlow the Mayor, but he seemed to be too much of a Patriot and Liberty Monger to be concerned about such matters.'[1] This comment explains how it was that the Cross was not considered necessary, and no more was heard of it, but even after this second one had disappeared, the custom of proclaiming the Sovereign from the site of the Cross continued. Queen Victoria was proclaimed there, as well as in the middle of the Market Place.

There were many disputes between Town and University with regard to rights over the Market. Queen Elizabeth, who granted many privileges to the University (although she never founded the College she had promised), ruled in 1561, that 'the Chancellor, Masters and scholars should only and for ever, hold the office of clerk of the Queen's market, in the town of Cambridge and the suburbs'; this state of things lasted until the reign of Queen Victoria, when on the recommendation of a University syndicate a comprehensive Act was passed in 1856, for the 'Settlement of Matters in Difference between the University and Borough of Cambridge'. It was then enacted that 'the privileges, powers, and authorities heretofore exercised by the university and its officers with respect to the markets and fairs of and within the borough be abolished'.

To return to Elizabeth. The Vice-Chancellor, Dr Roger Goade, having control of the Market, issued a rule 'that no students do walke upon the Market Hill or sitt upon the Stalls or other places thereabout, or make any stay at

[1] W. M. Palmer, *William Cole of Milton*, p. 71.

all in ye said Market place or elsewhere within ye Town, longer than they shall have necessary cause, being appointed by their Tutors to dispatch some necessary business'. The same Vice-Chancellor, evidently thought that discipline needed tightening up, for upon taking office in 1595 he had also made it known that 'no student was to wear long or curled locks, great ruffes, velvet Pantables, velvet Breeches, coloured nether stockes, or any other coloured apparell' and 'that the hurtfull and unscolerlike exercise of Football and meetings tending to that end, do from henceforth utterly cease'[1]—except as a concession in separate colleges—a rule which had been enforced by Dr Caius in his own College many years earlier.[2]

When Lord North became High Steward he had a scheme for building a Court-house for assizes and sessions in the Market Place, and to make space it was decided that all the fish-stalls should in future stand on Peas Hill. The Fish Market was important, and dealt in a great variety of fish: salmon, Colchester oysters, as well as mackerel, herrings, sprats, eels, jacks, and other fresh-water fish. The building was not carried out, but the fish-stalls were moved and evidently created a nuisance from their proximity to the residence of Dr Hatcher, who lived in the former Augustinian Friary, where Barclays Bank now stands.[3] Lord North, having originally caused the trouble, was again active, and urged the Town to accept £20 from Dr Hatcher for paving and penthousing the Fish Market at Peas Hill, presumably to abate the nuisance. This appears to have been done.

[1] Cooper, *op. cit.* p. 538.    [2] Venn, *Early Collegiate Life*, p. 62.
[3] See also 'Cambridge Waits', Ch. III, p. 72.

## The Guildhall & the Market Place

The Augustinian Friary, facing Peas Hill, later the home of Dr Hatcher, must have played an important part for 250 years in the history of the Town. It has been fully described by Dr Cranage and the late Canon Stokes in a communication to the Cambridge Antiquarian Society in 1918. The Friary had been founded about 1290. No chronicle exists—such as that of Barnwell Priory—nor any description of the extent of its original property, but there are many allusions to it in other records and numerous references in the fourteenth century to additions to its site by gift or purchase until eventually the Friary grounds covered the whole area bounded by Bene't Street and Wheeler Street on the north, Downing Street (formerly Dowdiver's Lane) on the south, Corn Exchange Street (formerly Slaughterhouse Lane) on the east, and Free School Lane (formerly Lurteburgh Lane, variously spelt) on the west.

Established in such a central position, it is not surprising that there was occasionally friction between the friars and the civil authorities—relations with the University seem to have been more cordial, since the *Grace Books* show that the Church of the Friary was often available for University purposes. It was not until after the destruction of the Churches of the Augustinian and Franciscan Friars that Great St Mary's began to be used for secular purposes by the University.[1]

Miles Coverdale, translator of the Bible, after having taken a course of study in the University, joined the Austin Friars in 1514, together with Dr Robert Barnes,

[1] See also 'A Town Plan for Cambridge', Ch. VII, p. 129.

( 11 )

a scholar whose zeal and learning gathered around him a band of other scholars and reformers. He became Prior about 1523. He was a man of courage and liberal views. When Latimer was forbidden to preach in St Edward's Church, he invited him to continue his discourse in the Church of the Augustinian Friary, and himself took Latimer's place—an action which eventually cost him his life.

The Friary was suppressed with many other religious houses both great and small about 1538, and passed into the hands of William Keynsham, who sold it ten years later to Dr Hatcher, Regius Professor of Physic, and Vice-Chancellor in 1579—one of the few Vice-Chancellors who have not been heads of Colleges. He was a man of considerable wealth, who lived in almost princely style in the former Friary. After the death of his grandson, Sir John Hatcher, the property passed in sections to various owners. Thomas Buck, the University printer set up his printing press in the principal building in 1632; the press seems to have remained there for almost a century. At one time in the eighteenth century, Cole relates that a certain Mrs Wigmore had a flourishing boarding school in the part 'where the gate belonging to the House lets out towards Pease Market Hill'. About 1760 Dr Richard Walker, Vice-Master of Trinity, bought the site and presented it to the University for a Botanic Garden. In 1786 the University leased the house facing Peas Hill, which had become ruinous, to Mr John Mortlock for 999 years at an annual rent of one shilling. A century later the site of the house was repurchased by the University and is now covered by the Arts Schools.

## The Guildhall & the Market Place

At the beginning of the seventeenth century there had been serious danger that the Town would lose a central portion of the Guildhall site, for in 1601 the University obtained from Queen Elizabeth a lease of the Town Gaol, possibly for use in connexion with the Vice-Chancellor's court. James I confirmed this grant in 1603. In 1605 a lawsuit for possession was brought by the burgesses, who founded their title upon continuous occupation of the premises for three and three-quarter centuries. The matter dragged on, with varying fortune, until in 1607 the University obtained an order for referring the cause to the Attorney-General and the Solicitor-General.

Mr Wickstede, the solicitor employed by the Borough Council, with pardonable satisfaction thus relates the issue:

> Mr. Attorney and Mr. Solicitor heard the whole cause in the presence of the Mayor and Aldermen and Councell of the Town, as also of diverse principal Doctors of the University and their Councell, insomuch that Dr. Barrowe, Solicitor for the University, was very violent and angry with Mr. Wickstede, Solicitor for the Towne, who little regarding him for it, there was an end of the cause, they the said Mr. Attorney and Mr. Solicitor thinking it not fit for the honour of the University to question so antient a Title...whereupon the Town ever sithence hath been quiet and doth enjoy the Jayle as formerly they have done.

The Attorney-General was Sir Edward Coke and the Solicitor-General Sir Francis Bacon, both members of Trinity College, and Bacon High Steward of the Borough ten years later.

The Gaol, which was the subject of this famous controversy, continued in use for almost two hundred years more. James Nield, a follower of John Howard the prison reformer, who, like Howard, visited all the gaols in the country, writing in 1802, described the condition of Cambridge Town Gaol as it had been in Howard's time. He said: 'There was formerly a room below for criminals called the Hole, 21 feet by 7, and above a room called the Cage. No court-yard; no water; no allowance [for food]. On my visit, August 1800, I had the pleasure to find the Cage had fallen into the Hole, and both were a heap of ruins.' Howard lived at Cardington in Bedfordshire, and it may have been in consequence of his representations that the Gaol had been removed in 1788 to a new building in the lane now called Downing Place. In 1829 another move was made to another new prison on Corporation ground, to the south of Parker's Piece. In 1878 this building, which was contained in an octagonal walled enclosure, was dismantled, and many of the bricks were used for the wall round Fenner's cricket-ground.[1] After that date prisoners from the Borough were admitted to the County Gaol, formerly on Castle Hill, the last of the Cambridge local prisons. The Shire Hall, built out of the excellent hand-made bricks of the former prison, now occupies the fine site.

Another danger arose thirty or forty years before the 400-years' old Town Hall was pulled down in 1782. The space in front was leased for 999 years, at a peppercorn

---

[1] In 1846 Fenner began to let his private ground to the U.C.C., who had until then played on Parker's Piece. The Club bought the ground from Caius College in 1892.

rent, to certain Trustees for the County for a new Sessions House or Shire Hall, a condition being that the Town should continue to have the use of the stalls and cellars underneath. A Shire Hall was accordingly built by the County in 1747, consisting of two Law Courts, constructed on open arches like the old Town Hall which stood behind it, and the two were connected by a wooden bridge spanning a lane called Butter Row, where the stalls for dairy produce stood.

In 1842, when new County Law Courts were built on Castle Hill, the lease of the site in front of the Town Hall was surrendered by the County to the Corporation of the Borough. This was most fortunate for the Borough, but unfortunate in that it involved the destruction of the massive gatehouse of the Castle, to make space for the new Courts. One of the two released Law Courts was turned into a Council Chamber, and the lower arches having been closed in previously, the Sessions House became the front part of the Guildhall.

But before this transfer was effected, the old Town Hall in the background and the prison had given place to a new building planned by a local architect, 'the ingenious Mr. Essex', consisting chiefly of an Assembly Hall and an Aldermen's Parlour.

When Essex built his Guildhall in 1782, there was no occasion to design a fine elevation, as it was hidden by the Shire Hall. It was, however, recorded in the Corporation Cross Book[1] that an inscription provided by William Cole had been placed upon a foundation stone. Cole also mentioned this in the fifty-first volume of his unpublished

[1] The earliest volume of the Town records.

MS. Collections in the British Museum.[1] He added that he did not know whether it had been used or not; he died before the building was completed.

The position of the stone itself had been lost, buried as it was out of sight, and it was feared that it might have been destroyed, but it happened that when the Essex building was being demolished to make place for yet another—the present—Guildhall, the excavators discovered the stone lying on its face in what was apparently its original position, about 18 inches below the floor-level. Under it was a sheet of pig-skin or parchment, which flaked as soon as exposed. Two small coins were found below the stone.

By a coincidence, Sir Owen Morshead, Librarian at Windsor Castle, without knowing of the discovery which had taken place, contributed a letter to the *Cambridge Review* in October 1937, in which he mentioned that the first two volumes of the Yale edition of Horace Walpole's *Correspondence*, then just published, were devoted to the correspondence with William Cole. Cole's inscription for the new Town Hall was mentioned in the correspondence, for he subjected its latinity to Walpole's criticism before committing it to posterity. John Merrill, Mayor of Cambridge, had invited him, Cole wrote to Walpole, 'to compose a short inscription, which the Corporation have a mind to be a corner stone, and hid in the foundation of a New Town Hall, which they are erecting this year, under the direction of Mr. Essex, and mean to put a few coins

[1] Cole bequeathed to the British Museum nearly 100 folios in his own handwriting.

Plate VI. Foundation Stone of Guildhall
built by James Essex, 1782

Plate VII. Guildhall by James Essex (later known as the Small Room of the Guildhall) Used as a Reception Room for the British Association Meeting in Cambridge in 1845

under it'. 'Hid in the foundation' exactly describes the curious position in which the stone was found.

The stone itself is peculiar. It has been described as coming from Barnack, a quarry long worked out, and must be much older than the building in which it was used. The dimensions are unusual for a foundation stone: 5 ft. 3 in. long, 18 in. wide, and 10 in. thick. It appears to have formed at some earlier period the threshold for a door, as cavities are clearly marked in which posts could have been erected. The late Dr W. M. Palmer suggested that it might have come from the adjoining 'stone house' of the Jew Benjamin—or, if another suggestion may be ventured, is it not possible that it came from the ruined Barnwell Priory, which in the eighteenth century was still being used as a quarry for material? Barnack stone was certainly employed in the Priory buildings, for in the sole remaining portion, the Cellarer's Checker (Exchequer),[1] while the walls are of rubble clunch, all the dressings are of Barnack stone, as are the springers of the arches.[2]

The stone is now safely imbedded in an interior wall of the new Guildhall. The inscription is as follows:

Faxit Deus / Ut haec nova Gilda Aula / Communitatis Villae / Cantabrigiae / in ipsissimo Loco / Veteris jam periclitantis / et ruinosae / posita / Resurgat in Honorem / hujus venerandi Municipii / et / Prosperitatem / Praedificata autem fuit / haec Domus Communis / sive Gilda Aula / per Communitatem Villae / Amicis faventibus / Joanne Merill / tunc

---

[1] See also 'Barnwell Priory', Ch. IV, p. 107.
[2] T. D. Atkinson's report communicated to Cambridge Antiquarian Society in 1891 by J. W. Clark, p. 237.

Majore Villae / Cantabrigiae / Anno Regni Georgii tertij 22$^{do}$ / Anno Domini 1782 / Jacobo Essex Architecto./

In the Corporation Cross Book, on the page next to the Latin inscription, is the following:

Attempted in English.

'God grant that this New Guildhall of the Corporation of the Town of Cambridge, built on the very spot where stood the old and dangerous fabric, may rise to the honour and prosperity of this antient Town.

'This House of Common Council or Guildhall was built by the Corporation with the assistance of their friends, John Merrill being at that time Mayor of the Town, in the 22nd year of the Reign of King George III, and in the year of our Lord, 1782.
JAMES ESSEX, *Architect.*'

James Essex deserves a special word of commemoration. He was born in Cambridge in 1720, the son of a local builder or 'joyner', who was employed on many important works, and received his education in the Choristers' School attached to King's College. The school was held in a brick building at the south-east end of the Chapel, which Cole (writing in 1776) described as totally neglected.

Essex must have had a very full life, for there is practically no part of the Town or University that does not show his hand, with varying success. Besides his work at the Guildhall, he rebuilt the Great Bridge, built Trinity Bridge, did work at Queens', including the wooden bridge, and at King's, Trinity, St Catharine's, Christ's, Emmanuel, Clare, St John's, Corpus, Sidney, Great St Mary's, the University Library, Senate House, Madingley Hall and

Cole's house at Milton. Nor was his work confined to Cambridge. He was employed in the repair of Ely Cathedral, Lincoln Cathedral and the tower of Winchester College Chapel. He also drew up *Proposals for publishing the plans and sections of King's College Chapel,* in fifteen plates with remarks and comparisons, and many designs for new buildings. The Cambridge Town Hall was one of his latest undertakings, for it was opened in May, 1784, and he died in September of the same year. On his memorial tablet in St Botolph's Church, can be seen the following inscription:

In a Vault / on the South side of this Church / Lies sleeping in a state of death /

.        .        .        .        .        .        .

James Essex A.S.S. Eminent for his / Skill in Architecture and Antiquities / who died Sept. 14, 1784. Aged 63.'

His manuscripts and drawings came to the Rev. Thomas Kerrich, who bequeathed them to the British Museum.

After the Essex building, considerable additions to the already composite Guildhall were made in the nineteenth century, including a much larger Assembly Hall, a Public Library, a Petty Sessional Court, and various offices. With the growth of the town, this medley of buildings proved inconvenient and wholly inadequate for the needs of the Council and the local government staff of a large and active Borough, with the result that in 1932 it was resolved to rebuild once again on the historic ground, which through the purchase of a number of old houses had by this time been enlarged to form an island site. Even with this addition there was no space for a set-back such as would have provided a dignified approach to the building, but by good fortune nothing had been lost, and no town could wish for a better position for its Guildhall.

After some unavoidable delay, the new building was fortunately completed and occupied in the summer of 1939, and became at once the centre of the civic life of Cambridge with its vastly increased activities and responsibilities during the succeeding years of war.

The Old Market Cross

# CHAPTER II

# THE OFFICE OF HIGH STEWARD OF THE BOROUGH OF CAMBRIDGE

WHEN Cambridge, in March 1943, elected a new High Steward of the Borough, many questions were asked about the duties, if any, of this officer and the origin and history of the office, questions to which no ready answers could be given. The following notes have been put together with the object of providing a sketch of the medieval background of the office which does not itself appear in English municipal life until the close of the Middle Ages. To this has been added a brief account of the holders of the office in Cambridge to the present day.

The development of the story involves a tentative inquiry into the constitution of the medieval borough in some of its aspects, an inquiry which to be successful would call for 'a very perspicacious Person who hath an intuitive Soul'—to quote the words of an anonymous writer of the seventeenth century. 'We shall have to think away distinctions that seem to us as clear as the sunshine; we must think ourselves back into a twilight.'[1] 'Each town has its history, and makes its independent contribution to Municipal History as a whole'[2]—a challenge to every municipality to trace its own history before the trail is lost.

[1] F. W. Maitland, *Township and Borough*, p. 11.
[2] Stubbs, Introduction to *Charters of the City of Oxford*.

## By-ways of Cambridge History

As Maitland points out in his Introduction to the *Charters of the Borough of Cambridge*,

during the Middle Ages the function of the royal charter was not that of 'erecting a corporation', or regulating a corporation which already existed, but that of bestowing 'liberties and franchises' upon a body, which within large limits was free to give itself a constitution and to alter that constitution from time to time.... Elaborate constitutions were established and after a few years abolished, and some of our boroughs had enough revolutions to satisfy a South American republic.

Ever since the Norman Conquest, and even earlier, there have been various types of stewards with duties of varying degrees of importance. The name 'Steward' has therefore a wide range of meaning; even its derivation is uncertain.

The Lord High Steward, or Seneschal, as an important legal officer of the Government, was introduced from the ducal house of Normandy—by whom the system had been borrowed from the Carolingian court—and took his place in the Royal Household in England at the time of the Conquest together with the cup-bearer, constable and chamberlain. All ministers of state, in England as on the Continent, began as servants of the household,[1] and in the gradual transfer of functions the main legal powers of the Lord High Steward were assumed by the Justiciar and later by the Chancellor. The office, having thus become one of dignity and honour without specific duties, was for a time hereditary in the house of Leicester. Meanwhile, by the thirteenth century, working household stewards

[1] Tout, *Chapters in Mediaeval Administrative History*, I, 8.

had largely replaced the dignified steward in his traditional position as head of the Royal Household, and, upon the accession of Henry IV, 1399, the higher office became merged in the Crown. From that time a Lord High Steward has been appointed only for special occasions, such as a Coronation or the trial of a peer, and in his official capacity has made no great figure in English history.[1]

By the reign of Edward I, the working steward as Steward of the Household, was taking a decided part both in politics and administration, and his activity soon extended beyond the limited sphere assigned by thirteenth-century opinion to the functions of a lay steward. He was still Judge of the Household Court, and it was on the judicial side that he came most into conflict with the public. The jurisdiction of his court was supposed to be confined to offences by members of the household, or committed within the territorial 'verge', that is within the limit of twelve miles from the royal person. This court, which came to be known as the 'Court of the Verge', travelled about with royalty, and the steward was frequently charged with trying to extend the limit of the verge, until no subject, dwelling within a day's journey of where the King might happen to be, felt himself safe against his encroachments.

Although the Steward of the Household was forbidden to hear common pleas, and Chancery writs were issued from time to time defining and limiting his powers, there were recurrent complaints of his having exceeded his

---

[1] Stubbs, *Constitutional History*, I, chap. xi.

rights in this respect. Cambridge had had an experience
—one among many—of this tendency, when in 1383 the
Town Clerk successfully claimed conusance of an action
for debt pending in the Hall of the King's House in
Cambridge before the Steward, John Montague, and took
it out of his hands.

A much more flagrant example occurred in the following year when Montague, ever eager to extend the
jurisdiction of the Steward's Court, heard a charge which
the two chief justices appear to have been unwilling to try.
John Northampton, Mayor of London, was by his own
clerk accused of treason, and was tried and condemned to
death by the Court of the King's Steward. Montague was
not altogether successful, for the Chancellor intervened
and the sentence was changed to imprisonment, but by
persistent efforts successive Stewards of the Royal Household did actually obtain a position of great importance
and influence over a long period.

There is to this day an officer of the Household known
as the Lord Steward, who presides over the Board of
Green Cloth and is charged with the duty of examining
and passing the King's household accounts.[1] This assembly
still has the responsibility of granting the Royal Warrants
so zealously sought after by business firms.

In addition to the Stewards of the Household there were
Stewards of the Royal Manors and of the Great Ecclesiastical Liberties and Franchises, but, however highly we
may be inclined to estimate the extent of royal and ecclesiastical property, it is difficult to overrate the quantity of
land which during the Middle Ages remained in the hands

[1] Tout, *op. cit.* II, 41 n.

( 24 )

of the great nobles.[1] They, again, employed stewards of their manors, whose qualifications and duties were outlined in *Fleta*:[2] he should be a modest and discreet man, guarding the interests of the Lord of the Manor in every way; experienced in the customs of the market, watchful over his lord's dues and other matters affecting his prerogative. Most important of all, he represented his lord in the Manorial Court, where he must be incorruptible in judgement.

Ecclesiastical Liberties and Franchises were extensive in East Anglia, of which some, including the Isle of Ely, were very ancient. In each there was a High Steward or Seneschal who, by the thirteenth century, had taken all the lay functions of administration off the shoulders of the Abbot. In Bury St Edmunds the stewardship was hereditary, but early in the Middle Ages the hereditary Steward delegated the actual work to a sub-steward who had to see that the numerous officials of the liberty did their duty. He also had judicial responsibilities, and in Bury he held the 'Great Court' which corresponded to the Shire Court in the rest of the country. He was responsible for levying all fines and dues owed to the King and 'should yearly make clear accounts in the King's Exchequer for all manner of things appertaining to the said Franchise'.

In Ely there is no trace of any hereditary stewardship, but the Steward appears to have been doing much the

---

[1] Stubbs, *op. cit.* III, ch. xxi, § 467. See also N. Denholm Young, *Seignorial Administration in England*, p. 66.

[2] A treatise probably written *c.* 1290 by a legal authority confined in the Fleet prison. Edited by Selden, 1647.

same work as in Bury. Changes came in the fourteenth and fifteenth centuries when the Shire Court was to some extent superseded by the new 'maid of all work', the Justice of the Peace, who in local government was to do for the Tudor kings what the Sheriff had done for the Angevin kings.[1]

The Borough of Cambridge had no Steward of any one of the types described above. At the time of the Domesday Survey it was an ancient 'burg', copyhold of the King, to whom a farm, or fixed sum, was paid annually. This fee was usually assigned to some lady of the royal family, and Cambridge became, therefore, a 'dower town'. On the marriage of Henry III, his wife Eleanor was endowed with the cities, lands, and tenements (including Cambridge), 'which had been usually assigned to the Queen of England'. Catherine, wife of Charles II, was the last English queen to hold the farm of the town, which in 1671 was purchased by Sir George Downing, and by the will of his grandson, another Sir George, passed into the revenues of Downing College.

The farm, or rent, was originally collected from the burgesses by the Sheriff of the County but, since this system led to burdensome extortion, the burgesses were, in the twelfth century, probably by Henry II, set free from the Sheriff and were themselves made responsible for the payment of the same amount direct to the King.[2]

From this time there is frequent mention of Borough

---

[1] Dr Helen M. Cam, *The King's Government as administered by the Greater Abbots of East Anglia*. Published by the Cambridge Antiquarian Society.

[2] Maitland, Introduction to *Borough Charters*, pp. xiii, xiv.

Courts in Cambridge presided over by the Mayor and Bailiffs, who held a session five times a year for suits concerning land and a court every week for personal actions. They were also prepared to hold from hour to hour a Court of the Gild Merchant to decide disputes between merchant and merchant 'according to the exigence of the complaint'.

Henry III and Edward II, when confirming earlier concessions to Cambridge, also granted increased powers. In 1327 Edward III introduced the modern system of appointment of Keepers of the Peace, who in 1360, when they were given the power to try felons, acquired the more honourable name of Justices of the Peace.[1] Twenty years later, Justices of the Peace were appointed for Cambridge, the Mayor being included in the Commission.

In order to safeguard the rights thus slowly acquired by the Borough for its courts, continual vigilance was required to guard against encroachment not only from the Steward of the Household, as shown above, but also from the officers of the University.

The organization of the medieval University was well ahead of that of the medieval Borough, having been deeply influenced by the example of the University of Paris; its officers were appointed by statutes which were little more than a transcript from Paris. The right to a High Steward was early won, since it is recorded that in 1418 Thomas Lopham was in office. The election of the High Steward was to be made 'in the manner prescribed for the election of the Chancellor', that is, by calling a Congregation as

[1] Report of the Royal Commission on the *Selection of Justices of the Peace*, 1911, p. 1.

soon as possible after a vacancy occurred, the election to be completed within a fortnight. The office was originally held, like that of the Chancellor, for 'two years complete' or for such length of time beyond two years as the tacit consent of the University permitted.

The first appointment of a Chancellor for life, and possibly, therefore, of the High Steward also, took place in 1504 when Bishop Fisher was elected Chancellor. Fuller writes:

> The University perceived it was troublesome every year to choose a new Chancellor; wherefore having now pitched on a person of much merit for the place (so that they could not change but to loss) this year they concluded his continuance therein for term of life, which act of the University was anno 1514 more solemnly confirmed.

Bishop Fisher continued in office until he was committed to the Tower in 1534, where his execution took place in 1535.[1]

The Court of the Chancellor, Masters and Scholars of the University of Cambridge, often called the Chancellor's Court or the Vice-Chancellor's Court, appears to have been established by a charter of 1305, when Edward I gave the University of Cambridge the same powers that Oxford enjoyed, including power to summon burgesses and other laymen before the Chancellor in all litigation that did

---

[1] In the course of the thirty years when Fisher was Chancellor, there were six High Stewards of the University, two of whom died in the year of their election, while the last, Sir Thomas More, went to the Tower and the scaffold with the Chancellor. *Historical Register of the University of Cambridge*, pp. 3, 18, 28.

not concern landed property. This grant received confirmation by Edward II and Edward III, while Richard II in 1383 specially confirmed by charter in definite detail the Chancellor's right to exercise jurisdiction over 'all manner of personal pleas . . . in which a master or scholar or scholar's servant or a common officer of the University is one of the parties', and to imprison convicted offenders in Cambridge Castle or any other gaol of the Town.

In 1561 Elizabeth went still further by granting that whenever any person enjoying the privilege of the University should be accused by a 'layman' at the assizes or quarter sessions of having committed treason or felony, the University might claim the prisoner, who would then be tried by its High Steward. Before each trial, however, a special commission had to be obtained from the Lord Chancellor to authorize the High Steward to try the offender, and this procedure was ultimately found troublesome and expensive. Consequently the High Steward of the University seems not to have tried any persons charged with felony later than the middle of the eighteenth century.

In 1828 Parliament conferred upon Justices of the Peace summary jurisdiction in charges of assault, and henceforward undergraduates guilty of assault were more commonly tried by the Justices than in the Chancellor's Court. In a memorial drawn up in 1852, the Borough claimed that the Court of the Vice-Chancellor and Heads of Colleges was very inconsistent with the spirit and genius of our free constitution. The proceedings were secret; there was no jury; the accused had no adequate previous notice of the charge. He was denied professional assistance, and was cross-examined by the judges who were his accusers also, and from their decision there was no appeal. The University Commissioners reported that the High Steward's jurisdiction had 'become in practice a merely nominal power', except in the Court Leet for superintending weights and measures. Accordingly the way was easy for the Cambridge Award Act, 1856, to provide that 'the right of the University or any officer thereof to claim conusance of any action or criminal proceeding, wherein any person who is not a member of the University shall be a party, shall cease and determine'.

Hence, the Chancellor and the High Steward of the University are now only competent to deal with legal actions in which both the defendant and also the plaintiff or prosecutor enjoy the privileges of the University.

Thus finally the privilege which kings had created and legislators were slow to remove was submerged by the process of time and the rising tide of municipal independence.[1] But it took nearly six centuries to bring it about, for the final difficulties between the University and the Borough were not removed until 1894, when amicable negotiations resulting in a private Act of Parliament put an end to certain powers of search and arrest on suspicion until then exercised by the University.[2]

It might be thought that these long-drawn-out disputes with the University and its scholars must have been unfortunate for the Town. Maitland takes a more favourable view. 'I think', he says, 'that both Oxford and Cam-

[1] Arthur Gray, *The Town of Cambridge*, p. 61.
[2] C. S. Kenny, 'University Courts', *Historical Register of the University of Cambridge*.

bridge had good luck....Materially the advent of the scholars meant to the burgesses a large demand for food and lodging. Spiritually it meant an example of organisation and a stimulating battle for right.'[1]

The date of the first appointment of a High Steward for the Borough coincides in a remarkable way with an important case at law between the Crown and the Town, which was heard before the King's Bench in the Easter term, 1529.[2] The property of a man condemned to death for murder, having been seized by the Mayor and Bailiffs as their right, was thereupon claimed by the Crown. The Attorney for the Town pleaded firstly that 'Cambridge is an ancient borough and one of the most ancient boroughs of the realm of England, and that the said borough and town of Cambridge are, and before time and from time of which the memory of man does not exist to the contrary have been, one body and one commonalty incorporate in itself'; further, that during the whole of the aforesaid time the burgesses have pleaded and been impleaded by the name of the Burgesses of Cambridge, as well as by the name of the Mayor and Bailiffs of the town of Cambridge, and that they have been, and still are, persons capable of purchasing and holding lands. The Attorney appears to have brought forward these points in order to show that the Borough had the right to plead as a corporation. He then proceeded to demonstrate that the right to the goods and chattels of felons had been admitted by Richard II and recognized by Henry VIII himself in his letters patent in the second year of his reign.

[1] Maitland, *op. cit.* pp. 42-3.    [2] Cooper, *Annals,* I, 325-6.

The decision of the King's Bench was given in favour of the claim of the Town, which was thus recognized as a Borough 'by prescription', that is, by ancient custom. According to Maitland, new ideas about the nature and origins of corporations were making their way into English law early in the sixteenth century. The canonists had been advancing a theory that incorporation must be the outcome of a royal charter, and, without this decision of the King's Bench, it may not have been clear that the corporate quality could be claimed on the ground of prescription.

The old boroughs, Maitland adds, were in no hurry to buy new charters containing the creative formula, and it was not until 1605, in the reign of James I, that the Borough, on the petition of Lord Ellesmere, then High Steward, obtained from the King a charter under 'our Great Seal of England', making it 'a body corporate and politic in deed, fact and name'. Since, however, it had already successfully asserted its prescriptive right to be corporate, the saving clause was added, 'whether before-time they have been lawfully incorporated or not'.

The first recorded election of a High Steward took place in June 1529, within a few weeks of the decision of the King's Bench. The reasons for the appointment are nowhere stated, and it may have had a twofold origin. Cambridge, with its newly acquired status, probably desired the support of an influential patron, such as the University already possessed. The Crown, on the other hand, may have felt it necessary to keep in touch with the boroughs through an official approved, if not actually

Plate VIII.  Lord Clarendon
After Gerard Soest
(*See* p. 44)

Plate IX. Sir Thomas Chicheley
From a portrait attributed to William Dobson
(*See* p. 46)

appointed, by the Crown.[1] At a Common Day held on 20 April 1686, being Hock Tuesday, an important term-day, a new code of orders for the government of the Town was enacted. The oath of the High Steward then ordained ran as follows: 'You shall swear that you shall well and truly execute the Office or Place of High Steward of the Town of Cambridge in all Things to the same Office or Place appertaining according to the best of your Power, Skill and Judgment. So help you God.'

But when we inquire what were the 'Things' apper-taining to the office at that time, we do not find them laid down even in general terms, the nearest approach to a definition being contained much later in the Report of the Commissioners in 1833, preparatory to the Municipal Corporations Act. It is there stated that the High Steward was a Commissioner under the Paving Act, and a Justice of the Peace, but did not act. He never, like the High Steward of the University, presided over a court or held any legal position other than honorary. 'The High Steward', the Report continues, 'does not interfere in the business or jurisdiction of the Corporation. He may in some sense be considered as the representative of the Borough in the House of Lords, being the customary channel of com-munication with that House.' He has also been the usual channel of communication between the Crown and the

---

[1] The creation of new Boroughs by the Tudors was probably adopted as a means of strengthening the influence of the Crown among the Commons. Edward VI, in his short reign, created twenty-two, some of them large towns, but several insignificant. Mary added fourteen and Elizabeth many more. Hallam, *Constitutional History*, I, 45.

Corporation, and has occasionally claimed the right to exercise influence on parliamentary or borough council elections, as is shown by the following instances.

In 1557 the fourth Duke of Norfolk, when High Steward, recommended a burgess to represent the Borough in Parliament, but the Mayor and Corporation withstood the request on the ground that the chosen burgess should be an inhabitant of the town, and the electors thereupon made an independent choice. In 1569 the same Duke of Norfolk resigned in consequence of his advice having been 'unworthily neglected' in the election of Mayor and Bailiffs. About this time there was a project on foot for uniting the two Corporations of the University and Town, promoted by the University and opposed by the Town. The Vice-Chancellor and Heads seized the opportunity to write to Sir William Cecil, the Chancellor,

that it had been lately signified to them that the Duke of Norfolk intended to withdraw his patronage from the townsmen in consequence of the contentions in the Corporation. They therefore petitioned Sir William Cecil that he would persuade the Duke to renounce the townsmen, if he had not already done so, and that he would induce him to adhere to his resolution, lest overcome by the solicitations of the townsmen, he should receive them again into his protection. This matter appeared to them so important that they sent Dr Chaderton as a special messenger, to whom they entreated him to give credence on their behalf.[1]

In spite, however, of this urgent message, the Duke was persuaded a few months later to resume office, Lord North,

---

[1] Cooper, *op. cit.* II, 242.

who became the Duke's successor as High Steward, being one of those pleading on behalf of the Town.

In 1614 Lord Ellesmere was more successful in exerting influence; his nominee as parliamentary representative for Cambridge was elected, the condition that the burgess must be a resident in the town being waived. Before the election the Mayor wrote to Lord Ellesmere:

Wee had our purpose to elect our Recorder and one Burgesse resident in the Towne. Howbeit in waightiest affaires the Towne hath received your longe & most honourable Patronage, So in this or any other thing else uppon your Lordshipps likeing and direccion known, I hope the Towne shal be ready to esteeme your honours desire as a Comandment to be observed.[1]

There are, however, few such examples, and in the main the corporation and the electorate preserved their independence, except during the decadent period at the beginning of the nineteenth century, in the evil days of the predominance of the Rutland Club, formed in political support of the Duke of Rutland.

With regard to salary, a fee of 40s. a year was customary until the middle of the seventeenth century, and the Town Clerk in 1833 stated that the terms of appointment provided for a salary of £6. 13s. 4d., which, however, was not actually paid. Although there were no definite perquisites, there was a steady flow of gifts. These occasionally took the form of a piece of plate, but more often consisted of pike and other fish from the fens. Sir Francis Bacon, at his first election, received not only the usual fee and

[1] *Ibid.* III, 61.

( 35 )

3-2

a purse costing 14s. to put it in, but also fish to the value of £13. 6s. 8d. Both he and Lord North more than once received a gift of ten fat wethers at a time. Sometimes these gifts were supplemented by other good things for the table, such as capons, mallard, larks, 'marchepayne and a pottell of ippocras'. There were also expenses of feasting on a rather lavish scale when the High Steward was entertained by the Corporation.

From the beginning, the custom has been to present the High Steward with a 'Patent' of appointment bearing the seal of the Borough. The Common Seal, which has been described as the most frequent sign of Corporateness,[1] was first made for Cambridge in the reign of Henry VI. Previously the Mayor had only had a seal for his own use. The new seal bore a beautiful design representing an embattled bridge of five arches and thereon an 'escochon' of France and England supported by two angels kneeling, with the circumscription: 'S. Communitatis Ville Cantebrigge.'

In 1573 the Corporation ordered that no office should be granted by patent except the High Stewardship. In 1675, however, Alderman Newton records in his *Diary* that 'at a Grand Common day William Baron had his patent for Towne Clarke then granted to him and sealed; before it was sealed he read it publiquely in the Hall'.[2] Whether Alderman Newton was correct in his statement or not, there is no trace of this procedure at a later date, and the order of Elizabeth still stands.

[1] Weinbaum, *Incorporation of Boroughs*, p. 21.
[2] *Alderman Newton's Diary* (1662–1717), p. 73. Edited by J. E. Foster and printed for the Cambridge Antiquarian Society, 1890.

## The Office of High Steward

The patent as now issued, with the present Common Seal of the Borough, grants to the High Steward the right 'to have exercise and enjoy the said Office for and during the term of his natural life'.

It has not been found possible to obtain a complete list of boroughs which still elect a High Steward. It is known, however, that the following have a right to the appointment and keep up the old custom. All that have been traced date the appointment from the time of the Tudors or the Stuarts.

These boroughs, with the earliest recorded date of the appointment of a High Steward, are as follows:

Cambridge 1529
Exeter 1537
Bristol 1540
Oxford 1553
Ipswich 1557
Gloucester 1558
Reading 1559
Louth 1564
Guildford 1580
Kingston-upon-Thames 1584
South Molton 1590
Newbury 1596
Evesham 1605
Hertford 1605
Retford 1607
Romsey 1607
Banbury 1608
Great Yarmouth 1608
Stratford-on-Avon 1610
Maidenhead 1611
Wokingham 1612
Hereford 1620
Abingdon 1630
Colchester 1635
King's Lynn 1664
Newcastle-under-Lyme 1685
Tewkesbury 1686
Southwold 1689

## HIGH STEWARDS OF THE BOROUGH
## OF CAMBRIDGE

1529. THOMAS HOWARD, *third Duke of Norfolk*, was elected as the first High Steward. Upon his election, the Town Clerk rode to London to convey to the Duke the patent of appointment 'sealed with the Comen Sealle'. The sum of £3 was received from the Treasurer, 'whereof payed, Fyrste to the Duke for his fee 40s. Item, for a purse to putt in the same fee 12s. Item, a box to put in the patent 1d.'[1] The further expenses amounted to 18s. and were disbursed as follows: the Town Clerk dined at Barkway, supped at Ware, breakfasted at Westminster, entertained friends at dinner at the Swan in Holborn, and spent the night at Ware on the homeward journey, with the result that he had to come upon the Treasurer for an additional sum of 10s. 1d.

The Duke, at this time High Steward of the University and President of the Privy Council, was a few years later ousted from royal favour by the Duke of Somerset and condemned to death. He was saved from execution by the death of Henry VIII, but was confined in the Tower throughout the reign of Edward VI.

1547. EDWARD SEYMOUR, *Duke of Somerset*, who was given the title of Protector, his nephew, Edward VI, being only nine years of age on his accession. He was appointed High Steward of England for the Coronation, and made Chancellor of the University of Cambridge in the same

---

[1] Borough Treasurers' Accounts.

year. In 1552, having been convicted of felony on what is said to have been slight evidence, he was beheaded on Tower Hill.

1552. JOHN DUDLEY, *Duke of Northumberland*, succeeded Somerset, his rival, whose death he had brought about. In the same year he was elected Chancellor of the University of Cambridge. Upon the accession of Mary Tudor, whom he had actively opposed, he was taken from Cambridge to the Tower of London and beheaded, only a year after Somerset's death.[1]

The third Duke of Norfolk, then released from the Tower, was reinstated, but died in the following year.

1554. THOMAS HOWARD, *fourth Duke of Norfolk*, succeeded his grandfather, the third Duke. In 1572, having planned to marry Mary, Queen of Scots, and thus becoming involved in Ridolfi's plot against Queen Elizabeth, he was executed for high treason.

1572. ROGER, *second Baron North*, popular both in County and Town, can be celebrated as the first of the High Stewards to be both a local man and interested in establishing a theatre in the town. He sat in Parliament for the County from 1555 to 1564, when he succeeded his father in the House of Lords. In 1568 he was elected Alderman and free Burgess of the Borough, and the following year was appointed Lord Lieutenant of the County. In the latter capacity he was in 1569 Commissioner of Musters and tried to conscript College servants, but was success-

---

[1] See also 'Guildhall and Market Place', Ch. 1, p. 7.

fully resisted by the University.[1] 'Fresh duties', it is recorded, were thrown on him by his appointment to the High Stewardship of the Town; and in the exercise of his authority he often came into collision with the University. The latter made a remonstrance as to the countenance which North—who was a great patron of players—gave to certain strollers who had performed at Chesterton in defiance of the Vice-Chancellor's prohibition.

He took an active part in supporting the claim of the Town to the control of Sturbridge Fair—a claim which the University had long been contesting. Matters came to a head in the reign of Elizabeth, and in 1577, when the townsmen presented a petition to the Queen for the grant of the Fair, she told them that she would not take away any privileges that she had granted the University, but would rather add to them; for which pronouncement the University duly returned a letter of thanks.

Lord North thereupon wrote a letter to the Corporation in the course of which, alluding to the danger to the interests of the Town, he said: 'When I considered the perill thereof,...I did acquaynt her Majestie with your case.... You shall not onely have me a friend but in this case a servant for the towne...and think me no ill officer.' The next year this promise was followed up by a stately entertainment lasting two days given to Elizabeth at Kirtling in Cambridgeshire, 'at my Lord Northes, who was no whit behind any of the best for a franke house, a noble

[1] In accordance with the Letters Patent of Elizabeth 1561, where it was laid down that the Chancellor, Masters and Scholars, and their Servants should not be compelled to appear for musters of men of war, nor be called upon to contribute to expenses of war.

heart, and well ordered entertaynement'. An inordinate banquet in the course of this visit included, amongst more solid fare, a cartload and two horse-loads of oysters.[1] Lord North's hope, however, of speedily getting a satis-factory settlement was disappointed, for it was not until eleven years later, in 1589, that the Queen made an effort to solve the problem and keep the peace by confirming to both Town and University all profits and privileges that had been granted to either of them for the previous twenty years—a solution that was no solution, for causes of friction still remained. Elizabeth's ruling was very un-welcome. So strong, indeed, was the resentment that at the foot of a transcript of the Borough Charter it is recorded:

One Gawnt was Maior of Cambridge, who att London assented to these new Jurisdictions of the Universitie, and therein betrayed the Towne, who shortlie after was putt [out] of his Aldermanshipp & lived the remaynder of his life in great want & miserie, & hatefull to all the townesmen.[2]

In 1588 it fell to Lord North to look to the condition of Cambridgeshire in preparation for the Spanish Armada, supplying a considerable force at his own charges. It was written of him:

There was none fitter to represent our State than my Lord North, who had been two years in Walsingham's house, four

[1] *Dictionary of National Biography*, based on information from the Municipal Records, supplied by J. E. L. Whitehead, Town Clerk 1887–1923.
[2] Sturbridge Fair was proclaimed for the last time in September 1933. See also, 'Cambridge Waits', Ch. III, p. 70.

in Leicester's service, had seen six courts, twenty battles, nine treaties and four solemn jousts—whereof he was no mean part—a reserved man, a valiant soldier, and a courtly person.

1600. THOMAS EGERTON, *Baron Ellesmere* and *Viscount Brackley*, Lord Keeper of the Great Seal of England and Lord Chancellor, was employed by Elizabeth on diplomatic commissions, and helped to determine the Act of Union between England and Scotland. While Lord Ellesmere was High Steward of the Borough, James I called upon him as Lord Chancellor of England to see to it that the Vice-Chancellor of the University should always take precedence of the Mayor. He was also Chancellor of the University of Oxford, and High Steward of the City of Oxford.

1617. FRANCIS BACON, *Viscount St Albans*, Lord Keeper, and Lord Chancellor, who had been befriended by Lord Ellesmere, succeeded him as High Steward. The Borough already owed a debt of gratitude to Sir Francis for action taken ten years previously, when he, being then Solicitor-General, was party to a decision in favour of the Corporation affecting the site upon which the Guildhall now stands.[1]

In 1614 Bacon had been elected a representative of the University in Parliament. He always kept tender feelings for the place and was accustomed to send his major works to the University Library, as well as to Trinity, with an accompanying letter. In 1620, three years after his election as High Steward, he sent this letter to the University of

---

[1] See 'Guildhall and Market Place', Ch. I, p. 15.

Cambridge upon his sending to their public library his
*Novum Organum*:[1]

Seeing I am your Son, and your Disciple, it will much
please me to repose in your Bosom, the Issue which I have
lately brought forth into the World; for otherwise I should
look upon it as an exposed Child. Let it not trouble you, that
the Way in which I go is new: Such things will of necessity
happen in the Revolution of several Ages. However the
Honour of the Ancients is secure: That, I mean, which is due
to their wit. For Faith is only due to the Word of God, and
to Experience. Now, for bringing back the Sciences to Experience, is not a thing to be done: But to raise them anew
from Experience, is indeed, a very difficult and laborious, but
not a hopeless Undertaking. God prosper you and your
Studies. Your most loving Son,

FRANCIS VERULAM, *Chancel.*

1626. THOMAS COVENTRY, *Baron Coventry*, Lord
Keeper. Being an enemy of Bacon and one of those who
caused his downfall, there was an element of disloyalty
and time-serving in the Town's appointment of him to
succeed Bacon. In 1629 he tried to mediate between
Charles and the Parliamentary leaders, but a few years
later assented to the levying of ship-money.

1640. JOHN FINCH, *Baron Finch of Fordwich*, Speaker of
the House of Commons, and fourth Lord Keeper in
succession to hold the High Stewardship, was elected in
February 1640. In March of that year and again in October

[1] *Baconiana* (1679), pp. 191, 192, there translated from the Latin
original.

he tried to obtain the election of his brother, Sir Nathaniel Finch, as one of the burgesses representing Cambridge in Parliament, on both occasions in vain. He himself was impeached in October in the Long Parliament, and two months later fled to Holland where he remained until the Restoration, then returning to England only to die. Meanwhile his post had been filled.

1652. OLIVER CROMWELL was elected in place of the absentee, Lord Finch. He was also High Steward of Bristol and of Gloucester. In his earlier career, he had of course been a man of consequence in the County, and was educated at Sidney Sussex College. But his association with the Town had also been close. In 1640 he had been made a Freeman of the Town, was elected as one of the two members of Parliament for the Borough and sat as member for Cambridge throughout the Long Parliament. On 15 August 1642 he seized the magazine in the Castle at Cambridge and hindered the carrying of the University plate to the King. In the spring of 1643 he made Cambridge his headquarters. He then engaged himself in fortifying the Town and timbered the old '*burh*' once more.

In 1654, having been proclaimed Lord Protector in the previous year, he was, as High Steward, presented with a piece of plate, since he was unwilling to receive money.

1660. EDWARD HYDE, *Earl of Clarendon*. After Cromwell's death in 1658, there was a vacancy until 1660, when Edward Hyde, afterwards the Earl of Clarendon, was elected. Doubtless the Town invited Clarendon to take up the office because he was an upright, sympathetic character, reputed to carry great weight with the King in the earlier years of the Restoration. But his close association was of course with Oxford, of which University he was Chancellor, and there is no record of him in connexion with Cambridge except his own account of how he had smallpox in Trinity Street in 1628, when he was twenty years old. He was accompanying his uncle, Nicholas Hyde, then Chief Justice, to the Cambridge Assizes and, following the precedent set a short time before by Coke and always since followed, they lay at Trinity. When

it was apprehended that he might have the smallpox, he was removed out of Trinity College, where the Judges were lodged, to the Sun Inn, over against the College Gate, the Judges being to go out of town the next day; but before they went, the smallpox appeared; whereupon his uncle put him under the care of Mr Crane, an eminent apothecary, who had been bred up under Dr Butler,[1] and was in much greater practice than any physician in the University, and left with him Laurence St. Loe one of his servants, who was likewise his nephew, to assist and comfort him. It pleased God to preserve him from that devouring disease, which was spread all over him very furiously.

At the time of Clarendon's election as High Steward, he

---

[1] A renowned and eccentric medical practitioner in Cambridge (1536–1618). He lived with Crane, to whom he left most of his estate. On his tomb in Great St Mary's the following words form part of the inscription:

'Abi viator, et ad tuos reversus narra te videsse
Locum in quo salus jacet.'

was Lord Chancellor and virtually head of the Government. He did not, however, escape the changes of fortune which befell several of his distinguished predecessors, and having eventually been overthrown by Court intrigues and the hostility of Parliament, he was banished in 1667. It was while in exile that he completed his *History of the Rebellion.* It has been said that Clarendon is remarkable as one of the first Englishmen who rose to office chiefly by his gifts as a writer and speaker, though the same might have been said of Francis Bacon, his predecessor in the office of High Steward. In his absence there was again a vacancy for three years.

1670. SIR THOMAS CHICHELEY, *of Wimpole,* in Cambridgeshire, Member of Parliament for the County, and subsequently for the Borough. It is recorded by Cooper that, on the 10th of January, the Right Honourable Sir Thomas Chicheley, Knt., one of his Majesty's most honourable Privy Council, was elected High Steward of the Town, which office seems to have been vacant ever since the passing of 'An Act for banishing and disenabling the Earl of Clarendon', by which that nobleman was disabled from having, holding or enjoying any office or place of public trust or any other employment whatsoever. Alderman Newton gives, in his *Diary,* further particulars of the ceremony of Chicheley's election. On 17 January

Tewsday at a generall Common day adjourned from the Tewsday before to this day, was the Patent of Sir Thomas Chicheley sealed for his being High Steward of Cambridge. The same day came in and were sworne Freeman Captain

Hunt and Mr Turner at the Rose;...they both together gave a Treat of wine at the Rose to the Mayor, Aldermen and 24[ty] &c.[1]

Later in the same year, Chicheley was consulted about a present to the King, who was expected to come to Cambridge while on a visit to Newmarket. He was asked if he thought fit that 'six score peeces of broad gold' should be presented to the King, and if the Queen came too, she should have '100 guynyes'. The Queen did not come and the present to the King finally consisted of '100 twenty shilling peeces of broad gold in a crimson coullered velvet purse with gold fringe and gold strings'.[2]

The occasion was the first visit of Charles II to Cambridge. After a ceremonial reception by 'the Mayor Aldermen and all Gownemen on Christs Colledge peece on the Greene sword', a procession was formed, some on horseback and some on foot, as far as the Regent Walk where the King was received by the University. Duty done, 'then I and the Aldermen', records our diarist,

went to the Towne Hall where wee had a very plentifull dinner at which were most of the Knights and Gentlemen of the Country, and dyned there alose my Lord Allington and Sir Thomas Chicheley the former is our Burgesse for Parliament the latter our High Steward. The Conduit run claret

[1] *Alderman Newton's Diary*, p. 59. In ordinances made for regulation of the Market in 1376 (Ed. III) mention is first made of 'the twenty-four lately elected in the name of the whole commonalty'. This was the body subsequently called the Common Council, though for several centuries they were as frequently termed 'the four-and-twenty', or the 24[ty]. Corporation Cross Book.

[2] *Ibid.* p. 63.

wine when his Majestie passed by who was well pleased with it. Sir Thomas Chicheley was pleased to come downe from London on purpose, the better to Countenance us, in our appearance.[1]

These loyal gestures on the part of the High Steward seem to have been forgotten in the following reign, for, in 1688, James II issued an Order in Privy Council removing Sir Thomas Chicheley from his position as High Steward. The King claimed the right to take this arbitrary action under a new Charter given to the Town by Charles II in 1685, after the Corporation had been induced to surrender previous Charters granted by Charles I and James I. By the new Charter Sir Thomas Chicheley, who had already been High Steward for fifteen years, was to hold the office for life, but there was a proviso reserving to the Crown the power of removing at pleasure the Mayor, High Steward and various other officers by an order made under the seal of the Privy Council.[2]

1688. HENRY JERMYN, *Lord Dover*, was elected High Steward as directed by the King in a letter to the Mayor dated May 1688: 'We will and require you forthwith to elect and admit Our Right Trusty and well beloved Councellor Henry Lord Dover to be High Steward in the room of Sir Thomas Chicheley.'[3] Dover was, however, not elected until July, and held the High Stewardship for a few months only. Upon James's abdication in December, Dover followed him to France and afterwards to Ireland, where he commanded a troop at the Battle of the Boyne

---

[1] *Alderman Newton's Diary*, pp. 64–6.
[2] Cooper, *op. cit.* III, 604.     [3] *Ibid.* III, 640.

in 1690. After the battle his situation was deplorable, as he had succeeded in making himself odious to both the Irish and the French. In his despair he threw himself at William's feet and was graciously assured that he had nothing to fear.[1] Henceforward he lived peaceably and retired at his seat at Cheveley in Cambridgeshire.[2]

Meanwhile, after Dover had left England, Chicheley was reinstated, and, when in 1689 representatives of the University and the Town were appointed to attend a Convention in London to confer about the succession of William and Mary to the throne, Isaac Newton and he were among the four selected.

1698. EDWARD RUSSELL, *Earl of Orford*, nephew of the fifth Earl of Bedford, later the first Duke. He had joined the service of William of Orange about 1683, and commanded the ship bringing him to England in 1688. In 1692 he was Admiral in command of the combined English and Dutch fleets which at La Hogue[3] defeated the French fleet collected by Louis XIV for the invasion of England in support of James II. For this victory he received the title of Earl of Orford. He was member of Parliament for the County in 1695, and Lord Lieutenant in 1715; impeached but acquitted in 1701. In 1705 he received Queen Anne when she visited Cambridge.

Lord Orford lived at Chippenham near Newmarket, and on his death his house came to Lord Sandys, who had

[1] Macaulay, *History of England*, III, 714.
[2] Cooper, *op. cit.* III, 639 n.
[3] Point de la Hogue, or Hougue, five miles north of Quinéville on the coast of Normandy.

married one of his daughters. In 1742, the Orford title was revived for Sir Robert Walpole, and that same year Lord Sandys was one of a Committee appointed to inquire into the new Lord Orford's conduct for supposed ministerial corruption.

1727. EDWARD HARLEY, *second Earl of Oxford,*[1] was a friend of Pope and Swift, and the poet, Prior, died in his house at Wimpole Park in Cambridgeshire. The famous collection of manuscripts made by his father and himself, including the earlier collections of Foxe, Stow and D'Ewes, and known as the Harleian Collection, was acquired for the nation and is now in the British Museum. In consequence of his extravagant expenditure, he had to part with the Wimpole Estate shortly before his death. (See also, Barnwell Priory, Ch. IV, p. 82.)

1741. HENRY BROMLEY, *first Baron Montfort*, Lord Lieutenant 1730, superseded 1742. Together with other estates, including one in Barbados, Montfort had inherited land at Horseheath in Cambridgeshire, where he built Horseheath Hall, of which all traces are now lost. Defoe[2] describes it as a lofty building, with large apartments, but domestic convenience seems to have been sacrificed to ostentation. It was approached by a 'noble flight' of steps, leading to a hall also of noble dimensions, 35 ft.

---

[1] A title which has been held by three different families: Vere, Harley, and Asquith. The Vere's held the earldom in an unbroken male line from 1142 to 1703, the twentieth and last Lord Oxford of the Vere family having had the title for seventy-one years. It was revived in 1711 for Sir Robert Harley, father of Edward Harley.

[2] Defoe, *Tour Thro' Great Britain*, 7th ed. I, 86.

square and 30 ft. high, having moreover on each side fine staircases occupying a vast amount of space. Montfort had many friends in the Borough and entertained on a large scale. His lavish expenditure and gambling propensities landed him in debt and he destroyed himself on New Year's Day 1755.[1]

Cole, in his *Diary*, writes of him thus:

He died suddenly *manu propria* on Jan. 1st 1755, at his house in London, leaving behind him, with those who knew him not, but an indifferent character, but with those who knew him more perfectly the character of a man of as much honour and integrity as is to be met with amongst the greatest examples of it. I knew him personally from a child, and notwithstanding the present clamour of the world against him, I declare solemnly that I would as soon have taken my Lord Montfort's word as I would another's bond.[2]

1755. THOMAS BROMLEY, *second Baron Montfort*, succeeded his father as High Steward within a week of the tragic death of the latter, being then only about twenty years of age. He, too, gambled heavily and in 1777 had to part with the estate, which had already been mortgaged by his father. The fine iron gates were bought by Trinity College. He continued to hold the office of High Steward until his death in 1799.

1800. JOHN HENRY MANNERS, *fifth Duke of Rutland*, who did not take the oath of office until 1818. The Rutland family had, in the middle of the eighteenth century,

---

[1] *Horace Walpole's Correspondence*, ed. 1840, pp. 93, 98, 145.
[2] W. M. Palmer, *William Cole of Milton*, p. 59.

acquired a large estate at Cheveley, near Newmarket. The fifth Duke took a leading part in the corruption of the Cambridge constituency, and in 1836 was removed from office by the Borough Council newly elected under the Municipal Corporations Act, 1835.

1836. FRANCIS GODOLPHIN OSBORNE, *Lord Godolphin*, a son of the fifth Duke of Leeds, lived at Gogmagog House, near Cambridge. He had represented Cambridgeshire in Parliament from 1810 to 1831 when he was created Lord Godolphin.

1850. CHARLES WILLIAM WENTWORTH, *Earl Fitzwilliam*, supported Parliamentary reform and was one of the earliest advocates of free trade. He edited Burke's *Correspondence*.

1857. THOMAS BABINGTON MACAULAY, *Lord Macaulay*, Fellow of Trinity College.

In the autumn of 1857 the High Stewardship of the Borough of Cambridge became vacant by the death of earl Fitzwilliam, and Macaulay was elected in his place by the unanimous vote of the Town Council. 'I find', he says in his Diary, 'that the office has been held by a succession of men of the highest eminence in political and literary history;—the Protector Somerset; Dudley Duke of Northumberland; Ellesmere; Bacon; Coventry; Finch; Oliver Cromwell; Clarendon; and Russell, the La Hogue man. Very few places have been so filled.'

The ceremony of Macaulay's inauguration was deferred till the warm weather of 1858.

'On Tuesday, May 11,' he writes in his Diary, 'I was at

## High Stewards of the Borough of Cambridge

Cambridge by ten. The Mayor [Mr Swann Hurrell] was at the station to receive me; and most hospitable he was, and kind. I went with him to the Town Hall, was sworn in, and then was ushered into the great room where a public breakfast was set out. I had not been in the room since 1820, when I heard Miss Stephens sing there, and bore part in a furious contest between "God save the King" and "God save the Queen". I had been earlier in this room. I was there at two meetings of the Cambridge Bible Society; that of 1813, and that of 1815.... The room now looked smaller than in old times.[1] About forty municipal functionaries, and as many guests, chiefly of the University, were present. The Mayor gave my health in a very graceful manner. I replied concisely, excusing myself, with much truth, on the plea of health, from haranguing longer. I was well received; very well. Several speeches followed; the Vice-Chancellor saying very handsomely that I was a pledge of the continuance of the present harmony between town and gown.'

Macaulay had good reason to shrink from the exertion of a long speech, as was only too evident to his audience in the Cambridge Assembly room. There was a touch of sadness in the minds of all present as they listened to the brief but expressive phrases in which he reminded them that the time had been when he might have commanded a hearing 'in larger and stormier assemblies', but that any service which he could henceforward do for his country must be done in the quiet of his own library. 'It is now five years', he said, 'since I raised my voice in public; and it is not likely—unless there be some special call of duty—that I shall ever raise it in public again.' That call of duty never came.[2]

[1] This was the Assembly Room of the Guildhall erected by Essex in 1782. The present Large Room was built in 1865.
[2] G. O. Trevelyan, *Life and Letters of Lord Macaulay*, II, 429–30.

His last public speech was, therefore, in acknowledgement of the honour paid him by Cambridge in May 1858.

1860. FRANCIS, *seventh Duke of Bedford*, elder brother of Lord John Russell.

1862. WILLIAM CAVENDISH, *seventh Duke of Devonshire*, Chancellor of the University, and founder of the Cavendish Laboratory.

1892. JOHN JAMES MANNERS, *seventh Duke of Rutland*, Chancellor of the Duchy of Lancaster, twice Postmaster-General. He succeeded his brother in the Dukedom in 1888, but was better known as Lord John Manners, when he was a member of the Young England group and figured in several of Disraeli's novels. He was the author of the famous couplet:

> Let wealth and commerce, laws and learning die,
> But leave us still our old nobility.

1907. COLONEL THOMAS WALTER HARDING, of Madingley Hall, near Cambridge. When High Sheriff of Cambridgeshire in 1904, he added to the Mayor's chain of office a handsome pendant bearing the arms of Cambridge. The Mayor's chain itself was the gift of Colonel Harding's father, who was High Sheriff of Cambridgeshire and Huntingdonshire in 1889.

1928. EDMUND HENRY PARKER, Mayor of Cambridge 1893-4. A partner in Mortlocks Bank, Cambridge, and later Vice-Chairman of Barclays Bank.

## High Stewards of the Borough of Cambridge

1929. VICTOR CHRISTIAN CAVENDISH, *ninth Duke of Devonshire*, High Steward also of the University.

1938. GEORGE DOUGLAS NEWTON, *Baron Eltisley of Croxton* in the County of Cambridge, sometime Chairman of the Cambridgeshire County Council and Member of Parliament for the Borough.

1943. JOHN MAYNARD KEYNES, *Baron Keynes of Tilton* in the County of Sussex, Fellow of King's College and of Eton. The twenty-ninth High Steward and the first born in the Borough, uniting in his parentage University and Borough, his father having been Registrary of the University and his mother Mayor of the Borough. Founder of the Arts Theatre of Cambridge and donor of the Theatre Trust, of which the Mayor and Deputy Mayor are *ex-officio* Trustees.

1946. GEORGE MACAULAY TREVELYAN, O.M., Master of Trinity College, Cambridge, previously Regius Professor of Modern History in the University.

In looking through this long list of High Stewards, it may be noticed that of the five appointed in the sixteenth century, the first narrowly escaped execution, while his three immediate successors, having also fallen from royal favour, were beheaded. The fifth, although a courtier and a politician, was more fortunate and managed to keep on terms with Elizabeth throughout almost the whole of her reign.

At the beginning of the seventeenth century came a succession of four distinguished statesmen, each of whom

( 55 )

was Lord Keeper of the Great Seal. In 1670 there began a series of High Stewards mainly with local connexions, of whom three in succession in the eighteenth century paid the penalty for their own extravagance and became bankrupt.

There were three who were also Chancellors of the University: the Duke of Somerset, the Duke of Northumberland and, more than three centuries later, the seventh Duke of Devonshire. Fuller, in his *History of the University of Cambridge*, seems to have overlooked Somerset, for, writing in 1634, he says of Northumberland that he held two offices 'which never before or since, met in the same person'.[1]

The Duke of Norfolk, first High Steward of the Borough, and the ninth Duke of Devonshire, elected just four hundred years later, were alike in being High Stewards of the University also.

Cambridge, which has, so far as can be ascertained, the earliest recorded date of the appointment of a High Steward, has maintained the succession, as shown by the above list, for more than four hundred years with rare and brief intervals, and illustrates in this way among others the continuity of its corporate life.

[1] Fuller (ed. Prickett and Wright), p. 250.

# CHAPTER III

# CAMBRIDGE WAITS & ORLANDO GIBBONS

FOR some time there has been an increasing demand for good music, greatly augmented during the war when it emerged in no uncertain fashion. To meet this need in East Anglia, with its scattered population, and in some of the East Midland towns, a Regional Council, fostered and promoted by the Arts Council, is in process of formation, having as its object the establishment of a permanent Symphony Orchestra. Such an orchestra would have Cambridge as its centre; it would serve the towns in the region from September to May, while during the summer it would be concentrated mainly on the coast.

With this growing interest in music for the community and the special attention given to Elizabethan music, it may be worth while to look back to the period, lasting for at least three hundred years, when 'Town Music' supported by the municipality had a prominent place in Cambridge civic life. It was a very different type of music, for symphony and string quartet were then unknown, but it developed into something exquisite of its kind, and in the later Elizabethan period Cambridge could claim an important share as the home and training ground of Orlando Gibbons, the brilliant son of one of the Cambridge Waits or musicians, who formed the Town Music.

The Waits, again, form a link with the still earlier minstrels, whose name they often share, and minstrelsy itself has had a long history. The general term originally covered a great variety of performers, including the *trouvère* or troubadour, the *versificator* or poet, the *histrio* (actor), and the *mimus* (pantomimist).

At the head of the profession in the eleventh century was the troubadour, often a man of high social standing, such as Taillefer, who led the Norman attack at Hastings, singing the Song of Roland and juggling with his sword. The traditions that Rahère, founder of St Bartholomew's Hospital, had been minstrel to Henry I, and that Richard I was discovered in his captivity by his minstrel Bondel, if not true to fact, show the position occupied by such persons in popular opinion. Master Henry, *versificator regis*, to whom Henry III made various gifts, may have been the last of the troubadours—unless Geoffrey Chaucer can be counted in their ranks.

The troubadour was primarily a composer and reciter of epic poetry, but there was also a popular demand for entertainment provided by the writer and singer of light verse, and for the player. All these forms of entertainment, both literary and dramatic, were usually accompanied by music. Sir Edmund Chambers indeed claims that nine-tenths of secular music had its origin in minstrelsy.[1]

An interesting entry in the Close Rolls of Henry III for 1260, arranging for the annual festival in commemoration

[1] Sir Edmund Chambers, *The Medieval Stage*, I, 58.

( 58 )

of Edward the Confessor,[1] calls upon the barons and
bailiffs of Dover 'to send to Westminster ten or twelve of
the better men of Dover, and a handsome boat adorned
with banners and furnished with youths and trumpets,
who can play on the river Thames below Westminster
to our diversion and that of others'.[2] Similar orders were
sent to Sandwich, Winchelsea, Romney, Hythe and
Hastings, which make it appear that these bands were
connected with the navy, although of the same character
as the minstrels still maintained by kings and nobles. At
the marriage of Princess Margaret (daughter of Edward I)
in 1290, no fewer than four hundred and twenty-six
minstrels, English and foreign, attended. Medieval account
rolls of the expenses of royal and noble households, towns
and monasteries, are full of payments, often lavish, to all
kinds of minstrels, players and jugglers.

With the disappearance of the troubadours, as the taste
for the long-chanted ballads and romances died out, there
seems to have been a gradual differentiation, and while
some minstrels became more highly specialized musicians,
dramatic performances took a separate form and have an
extensive literature of their own.

In addition to professional entertainment, the people
had always had their own revels, often in dramatic form,

---

[1] This festival was always celebrated with great formality, and the
new Westminster Abbey Church was consecrated on St Edward's
Day, 1269.

[2] I am indebted for the above reference to Dr Helen Cam.
More than 450 years later, Handel wrote his Water Music, which
was performed at a royal water party on the Thames and so pleased
the King, George I, that he granted Handel a salary of £400 a year.

and in the sixteenth century Village Plays were numerous, especially in the eastern counties. They are found to have been popular in Cambridgeshire at Bassingbourn; in Suffolk at Lavenham and Mildenhall; in Norfolk and Essex in numerous villages. The assistance of the minstrels was welcome for their music. This was a usual and a considerable item in the expenses. At a great performance at Chelmsford in 1562, the Waits of Bristol and no less than forty other minstrels were employed.[1]

There were training schools for musicians, especially in France.[2] In many towns, both in France and England, minstrels formed themselves into gilds. In London they had been incorporated in 1469, and the gild still exists as the Corporation of Musicians of London.[3] Canterbury had such a fraternity in 1526; that of Beverley certainly existed in the fifteenth century and was reorganized in 1555, when rules were made that members must be men of honour, 'waits' to some town or otherwise approved.[4]

In 1428, when Orleans was besieged by the English, before Joan of Arc appeared and raised the siege,

on the twenty-fifth of December in order to celebrate the Nativity of Our Lord a truce was called. As the two peoples had the same faith and the same religion, they ceased to be enemies on feast-days and courtesy was renewed between the

[1] Chambers, *op. cit.* II, 122, 140.

[2] *Scholae ministrorum* and *Scholae mimorum* can be traced to the fourteenth century. The titles indicate separate schools for music and for drama. Chambers, *op. cit.* I, 53.

[3] The full title, 'The Corporation of the Master, Wardens and Commonalty of the Art and Science of the Musicians of London'.

[4] L. F. Salzman, 'Minstrels', *Encyclopaedia Britannica*, 14th ed.

knights of the two camps each time they were reminded by the calendar that they were Christians. Noël is a joyous festivity. Captain Glasdall desired to make it a day of rest with songs, following the English custom. He asked Monseigneur John, the bastard of Orleans, and Marshal de Boussac, to be so kind as to send him a troupe of minstrels, to which they graciously agreed. The minstrels of Orleans betook themselves to the little Towers with their trumpets and their clarions and played to the English Christmas songs which rejoiced their hearts. The people of Orleans who came on to the bridge to listen to the music found it was fine melody. But as soon as the truce was ended, each had to look out for himself. For, from one bank to the other, the cannon that had been at rest launched their stone and copper bullets with renewed vigour.[1]

The name 'wait' as a type of minstrel first occurs in the fourteenth century. The wait appears to have been

---

[1] 'Le 25 décembre, pour célébrer la Nativité de Notre-Seigneur, on fit trêve. Comme les deux peuples avaient même foi et même religion, ils cessaient d'être ennemis aux jours de fête et la courtoisie renaissait entre chevaliers des deux camps chaque fois que le calendrier leur rapellait qu'ils étaient chrétiens. La Noël est une féerie joyeuse. Le capitaine Glasdall désira la chômer avec des chansons, selon la coutume d'Angleterre. Il demanda à Monseigneur Jean, bâtard d'Orléans, et au maréchal de Boussac, de vouloir bien lui envoyer une troupe de ménétriers, ce qu'ils firent gracieusement. Les ménétriers d'Orléans se rendirent aux Tourelles avec leurs trompettes et leurs clairons et jouèrent aux Anglais des Noëls qui leur réjouirent le cœur. Les Orléanais, qui vinrent sur le pont écouter la musique, trouvèrent que c'était grande melodie. Mais, sitôt la trêve expirée, chacun prit garde à soi. Car, d'une rive à l'autre, les canons reposés lancèrent avec une nouvelle vigueur les boulets de pierre et de cuivre.' Anatole France, *Vie de Jeanne d'Arc*, 41st ed. 1923, I, 153-4.

originally a watchman, whose duty it was to 'pipe the watch', that is to sound the hours at night on his 'wayte-pipe', while patrolling the streets. The Waits were therefore different in origin from the earlier minstrels, but like them developed instrumental bands, and were admitted into the musicians' gilds, and the use of the names 'minstrel' and 'wait' indiscriminately for musicians employed by many of the larger towns tended to obscure this distinction. Towns employing Waits were, among others, Exeter (1396), Norwich (1408), Salisbury (1409), Coventry (1423),[1] Hull (1429), Southampton (1433).

From early times it appears to have been customary for Town Waits, like the original minstrels, to take some part in pageants, public plays and interludes. They did so in Norwich in 1556, and twenty years later they obtained the permission of the Mayor's Court 'to playe such plaies and tragedies which shall seeme to them mete'. These performances seem, however, always to have been subordinate to their musical entertainments, of which the following is an example. In 1553 it was agreed by the City Assembly of Norwich that the Waits should have, on certain nights, permission 'to come to the guyldehall. And vpon the nether leades of the same Hall nexte the counsaill house shall betwixte the howres of vij and viij of the clok at nighte blowe & playe upon their Instrumentes the space

---

[1] 'Till 1942, when the City Council undertook the provision of holiday entertainments for the war workers employed in the city, there was in Coventry, after the Middle Ages, no municipal activity comparable to the maintenance of the waits.' Frederick Smith, *Coventry, Six Hundred Years of Municipal Life*, p. 61.

of haulf an howre to the Reyoysing and comforte of the
Herers thereof.'[1]

The musical equipment of the Waits was probably
developed gradually out of the simple 'wayte-pipe'. As
Professor Dent writes:[2]

The comfortable conditions of Elizabethan England made
it possible for instruments to be much developed. The primitive rebeck gave place to the viol, made in various sizes, the
sound of which recalled to Roger North[3] 'the harmonious
murmuring of birds in a grove'. It was a gentle instrument,
suitable for private chamber-music. For more boisterous
merrymaking and for dancing, as well as for the theatre,
shawms and sackbuts (hautboys and trombones), together
with trumpets, made a more penetrating 'noise'—'noise'
meant simply a band of music.[4]

In 1584 the Norwich Waits had 'ij Trompettes, iiij
Saquebuttes, iij hautboyes, and v Recorders', which are
described as 'beeyng a Whoall noyse'. As bodies of
Minstrels and Waits from different centres often met and
performed together, it may be assumed that the same
types of instruments were common to all.

Wind instruments were the only kind officially provided, and if an individual Wait wished to play a violin

[1] G. A. Stephen, 'The Waits of the City of Norwich', published
in *Proceedings of the Norfolk and Norwich Archeological Society*, 1933,
p. 9.
[2] E. J. Dent, Mus.B., Professor of Music in the University of
Cambridge, 'Tudor Music', published in the *Cambridge Public Library
Record*, October 1936.
[3] High Steward of Cambridge, see Ch. II, p. 39.
[4] Cf. Shakespeare, *Henry IV, Part II*, Act. II, Sc. iv: 'See if thou
canst find out Sneak's noise'. See also p. 66.

he had to find his own instrument. Edmund Roe, who was appointed a Norwich Wait about 1720, was evidently admired as a violinist, since the following verses on his playing were published in the *Norwich Gazette*:

> WHEN the Ingenious ROE
> Directs his Nimble Bow,
> And Artful Graces gives the Smallest String,
> I think Ten Thousand Nymphs and Syrens sing,
> To banish my Fatigue of Grief and Cares,
> With Wat'ry murmurs and Aethereal Airs:
> And if he does the Larger touch,
> The charming Melody is such,
> I think Apollo wakes his Sacred Lyre,
> Or that I hear the bright Cœlestial Choir:
> But when upon them all he Rolls and Ranges,
> Runs such Divisions, such delightful Changes,
> Such Sounds salute my more than ravisht Ears,
> As parallel the Musick of the Spheres.

A minstrel is mentioned in the Cambridge Treasurers' Accounts as early as 1425, in the reign of Henry VI, but there is nothing to show whether he was a resident or a travelling musician. In 1484 Cambridge certainly had its own band, although on a small scale, for together with robes for the Mayor and hoods for the bailiffs, payment was made for vestments for the 'Minstrels of the town'. In 1499 (Henry VII) three minstrels are mentioned and in 1511, when the name 'Wait' first appears in the borough records, four received payment for a performance; in 1567 there were five; in 1727 the number had increased to twelve.

Plate X. Orlando Gibbons

From a portrait in the Examination Schools, Oxford. By kind
permission of the Curators of the Schools

(*See* p. 57)

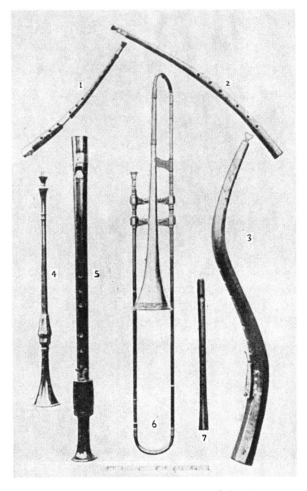

Plate XI. Musical Instruments of the Waits
Formerly in the collection of the late Canon Galpin

Special rewards for the services of the Waits were not uncommon, and this seems to show that their regular work did not constitute whole-time employment. In 1544, when Henry VIII's forces in Scotland took possession of Edinburgh, there is an item in the Cambridge Treasurers' Accounts: 'Payd to the wayts for goyng abowte the Towne with Mr. Mayor when Edenborowghe in scotland was wonne, iijs. iiijd.', and similarly later in the year when 'bullen [Boulogne] was wonne'.

In connexion with Henry VIII's military expedition to France, the third Duke of Norfolk, being then High Steward of both the University and the Town, had duties which might a little later have fallen to the Lord Lieutenant, and he was deputed to inquire from both bodies what number of 'tall and able men' they could provide to serve the King. How many the University provided does not appear,[1] but the Corporation agreed that the King should have 'twenty men out of the town at his voyage into France, whereof ten should be archers and ten billmen'. Voluntary contributions were invited for their outfit, and 'yelow clothe for the sojyers cotes' was provided—a forecast of khaki.

The share taken by minstrels was not always confined to peace parades, for some of the Norwich Waits actually accompanied Edward IV to France in 1475, and in 1589 Sir Francis Drake, having previously taken Waits with him on his buccaneering expedition round the world in 1577–80, and 'knowing how the pulse of men beats high to music', wrote to the Mayor of Norwich requesting

[1] In 1561 Elizabeth, by Letters Patent, exempted the University from all military obligations. See 'High Stewards', Ch. II, p. 40n.

that the Waits should accompany him on his expedition with Sir John Norris against Lisbon. A favourable decision was given in the Mayor's Court, and the Waits having been called into Court and all having assented, it was ordered that they should be provided with 'cloakes of stamell cloath',[1] a coarse woollen cloth, usually dyed red, and money to buy 'three new howboyes and one treble Recorder...and a Saquebutt Case'. Beyond besieging Corunna and pillaging the coast, the expedition accomplished nothing, but the mortality was high and only two of the five or six Waits survived.[2]

Sir Richard Hawkins also, in his *Observations in his Voiage into the South Sea*, A.D. 1593, describing his departure from Plymouth Hoe, says:

First, with my noise[3] of trumpets, after with my waits, and then with my other music, and lastly with the artillery of my ships, I made the best signification I could of a kind farewell. This they answered with the waits of the town and the ordnance on the shore, and with shouting of voices; which with the fair evening and silence of the night were heard a great distance off.

To return to Cambridge: we find that the local Waits, being a small band, were frequently supplemented by minstrels from outside. They came from neighbouring towns—Ipswich, Thetford (where there was a band of considerable fame) and Bury St Edmunds—or were lent by the King or Queen, or members of the nobility, who still had their own private bodies of minstrels. Sometimes

[1] Corresponds to Fr. *estamel*. (*Oxford English Dictionary*.)
[2] G. A. Stephen, *op. cit.* pp. 13, 14.
[3] See also pp. 63, 69.

they accompanied their masters; sometimes they seem to have been brought in to celebrate some special occasion.

In 1491, a year when Henry VII came to Cambridge, a number of entries occur:

Expences of the Minstrels of the Lord the King at the house of John Wighton [Mayor of Cambridge] this year 4d.

In expences of the Minstrels of the Lady the Queen...this year 6d.

In red wine given to the Minstrels of the Lady the mother of the Lord the King [Margaret, Countess of Richmond] this year, 5d.

In rewards given to the Minstrels of the Lord the King this year, about the feast of Saint Mary Magdalen, 6s. 8d.; and in rewards given to the minstrels of the Lady the Queen this year 5s.

All Waits wore a livery when on duty, and the Treasurers' Accounts mention many grants for the material for their cloaks. There is some uncertainty as to the colour of these official garments. In Cambridge they are described sometimes as 'tawney', sometimes as 'woollen cloth of a bloody colour'. It seems probable that the latter was not blood-red, since, in an entry in the Chamberlains' Accounts (1474) in Norwich, 'sanguinei' is crossed through and 'blodii' (blue) written above it. Further, in a Minute Book (1468) the colour is defined as 'blodii coloris videlicet tinctura vini' (wine-colour).[1] From the periods of the year when the payments were made in Cambridge, it is evident that the colour of the liveries was mixed tawny in summer, and russet, or tawny, or 'blodius' in winter.

[1] G. A. Stephen, *op. cit.* pp. 50–1.

With these cloaks, the Waits wore silver collars or chains, and silver 'scuttchins'. The latter were escutcheons or badges, worn on the sleeve. None of these decorations has survived in Cambridge, but beautiful collars and badges are still to be seen among the civic regalia in Norwich. There are specimens also in Bristol, Exeter, and York, and at King's Lynn and Leicester. The Norwich collars date from 1535, and were fortunately handed over to the care of the City Chamberlain before the fatal expedition with Sir Francis Drake in 1589, when so many of the Waits failed to return. The collars of the Cambridge Waits must have been of a still earlier date, for in the Treasurers' Accounts for 1499 there is an item of 21*d*. paid to John Banester 'for repairing the collars of the wayts'.

References to the Cambridge Waits recur in the seventeenth and eighteenth centuries. They took an active part, in 1660, at the proclamation of Charles II, when

the Vice-chancellor & all the Doctors in Scarlet Gowns the Regents and Non Regents & Bacchellors in their hoods turned & all the Schollars in Capps went with lowd Musick before them to the Crosse on the Market Hill. The Vicechancellor Beadles & as many D^rs as could stood upon the severall Seats of the Crosse, & the School Keeper standing near them made 3 O yeis.... The Musick brought them back to the Schooles again & there left them, & went up to the top of King's College Chapell, where they played a great while.[1]

In 1664, in the same reign, the Waits received a payment 'when the Lord Chancellor was in Towne', and again in

[1] MS. Baker, xxxiii, 337; xlii, 229. Quoted by Cooper, *Annals of Cambridge*, III, 478.

1685 'for playing when the Chartre was read'. This Charter, reserving to the Crown the power of removing at pleasure the Mayor, High Steward, Recorder, and members of the Common Council, cannot have been very welcome. It replaced other Charters granted by Charles I and James I, which the Corporation had been induced to surrender.[1]

In 1689 King William paid a visit to the town, and the Corporation, anxious to give evidence of their allegiance to the new Royal House, presented him with 'a bason and Ewer of about y$^e$ value of 33$^{ll.}$ brought down by John Disbrow goldsmith from London who was sent up thither to buy a cup of about 50$^{ll.}$ value but it could not be had'. Mr Pepys, the Mayor, gave the Waits £2 for their services on this occasion.[2]

In 1761, on the declaration of war with Spain, a great noise[3] was made with the Bellman and cryer on horseback, the waits, French horns and four drums, all being liberally paid, especially the waits.[4]

The Corporation went in procession with great splendour to proclaim Sturbridge Fair in 1727. The Crier in Scarlet on Horseback led the way, followed by the Town Music, that is the Waits, twelve in number with their banners[5] and streamers, the largest number of Waits recorded. There were in addition three drums, two trumpets,

[1] See also 'High Stewards', Ch. II, p. 48.
[2] *Alderman Newton's Diary*, p. 103.       [3] See also pp. 63, 66.
[4] W. M. Palmer, *Cambridge Borough Documents*, pp. xlvii–xlviii (from volumes lettered 'Rentals').
[5] Every instrument carried by the Waits had a small silk banner attached to it.

two French horns, followed by many official persons on horseback too numerous to describe. The Mayor, however, cannot be omitted. He was in his robes mounted on a horse richly caparisoned, decorated with some of the finery of an earlier Lord Mayor of London, and led by two footmen called red-coats carrying white wands. Such a procession was, according to Cooper, continued annually till about 1758, when it began to be abridged, 'owing as it is said to the trouble and charge of keeping it in a suitable condition'. In 1790 the procession of the Corporation as a whole was discontinued and the fair was proclaimed by the Mayor, Bailiffs, and Town Clerk only. With changed conditions of trade and transport, the importance of the fair had gradually diminished, but the proclamation was continued each year until 1933, when the ceremony was performed for the last time, by the present writer, accompanied only by the Clerk of the Peace and the Sergeant-at-Mace.[1] The audience, who were solemnly exhorted to keep the peace and obey the rules of the fair, consisted of a couple of women with babies in their arms; the stalls, of which there were whole streets in the earlier days, were represented by an ice-cream barrow with the legend: 'Stop me and Buy One.'

The importance of the Cambridge Waits appears to have waned along with that of Sturbridge Fair, and it is probable that they did not continue as the Town Music after the disappearance of the Sturbridge procession in 1790, possibly for the same reason of economy. In that

[1] The proclamation was discontinued by a resolution of the Borough Council, approved by the Secretary of State in an order dated 5 July 1934.

year the Norwich Waits were disbanded, as a 'small measure of municipal economy'.[1]

While the Norwich Waits were still City musicians, the custom was established 'of their going about y^e City with their Musick, from Hallowmass to Christmass, playing under y^e windows of all good Citizens and bidding y^m good morrow by name.... And in Christmas time they go about dayly, to receive y^e Benevolence of y^e Citizens for y^e same.' This custom was widely spread and may have led to itinerant Christmas Carol singers being called Waits in the nineteenth century.

In the reign of Elizabeth, whose love of pageantry fostered and encouraged the development of public music, there appeared in Cambridge a musician named William Gibbons. Two hundred years earlier there had been a Mayor of Cambridge named Gybbon, but as the name does not occur in the Treasurers' Rolls of receipts and payments 1514, or among payers of poll tax 1512, or rentals 1561-2, quoted by Dr Palmer,[2] it seems probable that William Gibbons was not a native of the place. It happened that in preparation for the Queen's visit to Cambridge in August 1564, the Proctors of the University of Oxford, by special command of that University, were sent to Cambridge for the occasion, together with their principal Bedell, as related by Matthew Stokys, Registrary of the University of Cambridge, 1558-91. They came, he said, 'to see and hear, as near as they could, for their better instructions (if it should fortune the Queen's Majestie to

---

[1] G. A. Stephen, *op. cit.* p. 70.　　[2] W. M. Palmer, *op. cit.*

visit that Universitie) all our doings, order and proceedings'.[1] It is probable, as will be shown later, that Gibbons came to Cambridge about the same time, possibly accompanying the delegation, and he may have been engaged as a Wait to strengthen the Town Band, which was certainly increased in that year, since payments were made by the Treasurers of the Town for making two new Waits' collars.

William Gibbons married a Cambridge woman who had as her dower a house in St Edward's parish, which they sold in 1573 to Dr John Hatcher,[2] and the Gibbons family then moved into the parish of Holy Trinity. In 1567 it appears from an entry in the Common Day Book of the Cambridge Corporation that William Gibbons was appointed leader of the Town Waits, for

in the tenth year of our sovereign ladie Quene Elizabeth, Mr. Maior did delyver to William Gibbons musitian fyve sylver collers called the waites Collers, ponderinge xxvij oz. id. And the said William Gibbons hathe found sureties for the delyverye of the same collers agayne when they be required.[3]

Gibbons had a large family. His eldest child, Richard, who died in infancy, was buried in Great St Mary's Churchyard in July 1566, just two years after his father's presumed arrival in Cambridge. A second son, Edward, and two daughters were born in St Edward's parish, and after the family moved into the parish of Holy Trinity,

[1] Printed in Francis Peck's *Desiderata Curiosa*, and also in Nichols's *Progresses of Queen Elizabeth*.
[2] See also Ch. I, p. 10.
[3] Corporation Common Day Book, 25 November 1567.

another son, Ellis, was born, followed by three daughters, all baptized at Holy Trinity.

As the second surviving child was called Ellis, a name which with varied spelling (Ellys, Elise, Elice, Elyse) recurs frequently in the Rent and Poll Tax lists of that period, the supposition may perhaps be permitted that the name of the child was that of Mrs Gibbons' family. In 1574, Gibbons signed the Vestry Book at Trinity Church, and although in 1576, on 1 June, the Proctors complained to the Vice-Chancellor that William Gibbons did 'upholde, maintain, and kepe or cause to be kept a dansing schole within the Town of Cambridge', and Gibbons confessing the charge was fined 40s.,[1] it seems to have been regarded as a pardonable offence on the part of a man who had several small children to support, and, in 1578, he again appears as a vestryman.

Three of Gibbons' sons inherited their father's musical ability in varying degree. Edward, the eldest surviving son of the family, became a lay clerk at King's in the Annunciation term 1592-3 and was made Informator or Master of the Choristers the following Michaelmas term. He seems to have left Cambridge in 1598 for Bristol, where he had an appointment as organist at the Cathedral, and from 1611 to 1644 he was a priest-vicar of Exeter Cathedral. His manuscript compositions are preserved in the Music School, Oxford, where, as well as at Cambridge, he received the degree of Mus.B. His brother, Ellis, was also a musical composer; his name appears as one of the twenty-six musicians who contributed madrigals, 1603, in *The Triumphs of Oriana*, in honour of Queen Elizabeth,

[1] Cooper, *op. cit.* v, 305.

( 73 )

but beyond these two madrigals no other compositions attributed to him have survived. Canon Fellowes ventures the suggestion that they were in reality the work of Orlando, then a mere youth.

There were two younger sons, who came at the end of the long family—Ferdinando and Orlando—and it is with the youngest of all, and by far the most distinguished, that we are chiefly concerned. Surprise has sometimes been expressed that Gibbons should have chosen such an unusual name as Orlando for his youngest son, so much out of keeping with the general run of the family names—Edward, Susan, Mary, Elizabeth and Jane. If the name is taken in conjunction with that of the brother next above Orlando in age—Ferdinando—the following suggestion may provide a clue.

There was in Belgium a Flemish musical composer almost exactly contemporary with William Gibbons. His name was Orlando di Lasso. He had been in England as a young man in 1554, and soon afterwards produced his first book of motets in Antwerp. Later in life, when working in Munich, he wrote six Masses. After his death, his two sons, both good musicians, published in six volumes no less than 516 of their father's sacred and secular motets.[1] One of these sons was named Ferdinando. Even if there was no personal contact between Orlando di Lasso and Gibbons, the latter may very well have known and admired the productions of a contemporary, whose musical reputation had spread throughout Europe, and who was living when Gibbons' sons, Ferdinando and Orlando, were born.

[1] Grove, *Dictionary of Music and Musicians.*

## Cambridge Waits & Orlando Gibbons

There has long been doubt as to Orlando Gibbons' birthplace. Cambridge claimed the honour and has never definitely relinquished the claim,[1] but about a century after his birth Anthony Wood, the Oxford antiquary, mentioned that he had found an entry of the baptism of Orlando Gybbins in the register of St Martin's Church, Oxford (now incorporated with All Saints), on 25 December 1583.[2]

No mention can be found in Cambridge records of William Gibbons or any member of his family from April 1580, when his daughter Jane was baptized in Holy Trinity Church, until 1590. It has hitherto been assumed that Gibbons continued to live in Cambridge during that period, and that his residence there was uninterrupted from the time of his first settlement until his death in 1595. But the *City of Oxford Records*, a source of information which has apparently been overlooked, tell a different tale.[3] In these records there is clear evidence that Gibbons settled in Oxford in 1583, and became a householder, having taken a lease of the former Priory of the Augustine Friars for twenty-one years, at a rental of £10. The deed was made out to William Gybbons, musician, and was dated 21 December 1583, a few days before Orlando's

[1] His statuette was placed with those of seven other distinguished natives of Cambridge on the Conduit in the Market Place erected in 1855.

[2] A. Wood, *Fasti Oxonienses*, ed. Bliss, 1, 404. This discovery led Fuller Maitland to propound in his article in the *D.N.B.* the extraordinary theory that there were two musicians named Orlando Gibbons living at the same time, one in Oxford, the other in Cambridge.

[3] *City of Oxford Records*, 1509–83, edited by W. H. Turner, 1880.

baptism at St Martin's.[1] A year later, William Frere sold to the city the site of the priory and the fair and the tenements occupied by William Gybbons and others. This property afterwards formed part of the site of Wadham College.

Further, Gibbons clearly became one of the City Waits. There is an entry in the *City Records* for 14 September 1588:

> Hit is agreed that George Bucknall being appointed to be [one of] the waits for this citie, shall have the three scuttchins delivered unto him, which Mr. Gybbons brought in, and... Mr. Gybbons is to make one more to be likewise delivered to the said George.

It was very natural that William Gibbons should have accepted an appointment in Oxford, since his father must almost certainly have been living there at the time. From the *City of Oxford Records* it appears that a certain Richard Gibbons was admitted as a Hanaster or Freeman in 1549–50, and when William was admitted in 1582–3 he was still included in the list. In September 1562 he had been in disgrace with the City Council for 'heynous words spoken openly before the hole Counseyll', and 'shall be dismissed this house'. It seems, however, to have been a momentary lapse, for at the Council meeting the following month,

> Richard Gybbons, upon his umble submyssion beinge sorye for his offence heretofore comytted in this house, was this day receyved agayne to be accouncell wᵗʰ the Mayer, and was presently sworne to the Mayers Counseyll.

[1] *Oxford City Properties*, edited by H. E. Salter, 1926.

This departure from correct behaviour was evidently forgiven and forgotten, for in 1569 Richard Gibbons was elected as one of the two Chamberlains appointed annually from among the common council men to be responsible for keeping the accounts of the City.

William Gibbons was admitted to the freedom of the City on a small fee, as the son of a freeman, and it may therefore be presumed that his father was Richard Gibbons, the only one of that name on the list of freemen. Some slight corroboration is supplied by the fact that the name Richard was given by William to his first child.

Shortly after delivering up the badges of the Oxford Waits in 1588, William Gibbons and his family appeared again in Cambridge. The Bursar's Accounts in the 'Mundum Books'[1] at King's College show that in 1590 and afterwards from time to time until 1603 'Mr. Gibbons' was employed for musical performances on special occasions. William Gibbons died and was buried at Cambridge in 1596, and it is probable that all these entries refer to his son Edward. In 1598 and 1600 respectively two of Edward's sisters were married at Holy Trinity Church, where they had been baptized as infants. In 1603 William Gibbons' widow died and was buried at Holy Trinity.

His youngest son, Orlando, entered the choir of King's College in February 1596, at twelve years of age, and two years later matriculated as a sizar.[2] His subsequent career is well known. He was appointed organist of the Chapel Royal in 1605 and, in addition, he was made organist of Westminster Abbey in 1623. 'A glimpse of this great man

---

[1] King's College, 'Mundum Books', vol. xxi.
[2] Venn, *Matriculations* and *Alumni*.

at work in the Abbey' is afforded by John Hacket[1] in his description of the visit of the French envoys to make preliminary arrangements for the betrothal of Charles, then Prince of Wales, to Princess Henrietta Maria of France. On entering the 'Door of the Quire', Hacket tells us, they heard the organ 'touch'd by the best Finger of the Age', that of Orlando Gibbons.

After the marriage of Charles and Henrietta Maria had taken place in Paris in May 1625, Orlando, who with the Chapel Royal[2] had been summoned to Canterbury to receive the Queen, is said to have composed special music for the occasion. In Canterbury he was suddenly taken ill and died there at forty-two years of age. In his short life he had produced numerous musical compositions. He was concerned in 1611 with Dr John Bull and William Byrd in the composition of a music book for the Virginal, entitled *Parthenia*, to which he contributed the remarkable fantasia, *The Lord of Salisbury his Pavin*. In 1612 he published madrigals of five parts, for voices and viols. Sir John Hawkins, in his *General History of Music*, 1776, says: 'the characteristic of his music is fine harmony, unaffected simplicity, and unspeakable grandeur.' Many services and anthems of his are still in use; the Service in

[1] John Hacket, 1592–1670, Chaplain to Lord Keeper Williams, Bishop of Lichfield and Coventry, Member of Trinity College, Cambridge; left his books to the University. Chief work *Scrinia Reserata*, a Life of Archbishop Williams, not published until 1693.

[2] A term including not only the whole personnel of the establishment but the vestments, ornaments, and everything belonging to it. The custom of taking the whole of the Chapel Royal when the Sovereign travelled in state was old established. Fellowes, *op. cit.* pp. 40–1.

F and his anthem of 'Hosanna' are mentioned with great approbation by writers on music, and so, indeed, is his church music in general. He received the degrees of Mus.B. at Cambridge and Mus.D. from Oxford University, the Oxford honour said to have been conferred on him at the request of William Camden on the day when the latter founded the Chair of History at Oxford in May 1622.[1]

The Gibbons family may have had a long connexion with Oxford, for in 1435 a certain John Gebone was one of the jury summoned at the Exchequer to decide whether members of the University had been duly assessed for the subsidy by Thomas Chace, late Chancellor. They also appear to have been connected with the family of Guybon or Gebon of King's Lynn, who were living there in the time of Edward II and for many generations afterwards, since the Guybon coat of arms appears on Orlando's monument in Canterbury Cathedral, and, as Canon Fellowes points out, it was unusual at that date to adopt a coat of arms without a substantial claim.

This monument, erected to his memory by 'Elisabeth his wife, who bare him seven children', has an elaborate Latin inscription, beginning with the words: 'Orlando Gibbonio Cantabrigiae inter Musas et Musicae nato', which may be translated: 'To Orlando Gibbons born at Cambridge among the Muses and born for Music.' Unfortunately, the space left for the date of his birth was never filled in. It is clear, however, that the family

[1] Fuller Maitland says that Orlando Gibbons also received an Oxford M.A. by incorporation. If this is correct, he must have been previously M.A. (Cantab.).

tradition held Cambridge to be his birthplace, while his baptism may have been deferred until it could take place in his father's home town. It should be remembered that Edward Gibbons was a priest-vicar of Exeter Cathedral at the time of Orlando's death and was therefore available for information. As he was fifteen years older than Orlando, he must have remembered the place of his brother's birth and would hardly have allowed a mis-statement on the monument in Canterbury Cathedral, even if he could not supply his exact age for the inscription.

A glimpse of the next generation of the Gibbons family is given by John Evelyn, who took his wife to Oxford in 1654. Their sight-seeing led them to Magdalen College, and there in the Chapel, says Evelyn, 'was still the double organ...Mr. Gibbons, that famous musician, giving us a taste of his skill and talents on that instrument',[1] just as John Hacket, when Chaplain to the Lord Keeper, and acting as guide to the French envoys, had heard Orlando playing the organ at Westminster Abbey thirty years earlier. The performer this time was Christopher, elder son of Orlando, organist to Charles II and, like his father, a Mus.D. of Oxford.

[1] *The Diary of John Evelyn*, Globe ed. p. 176.

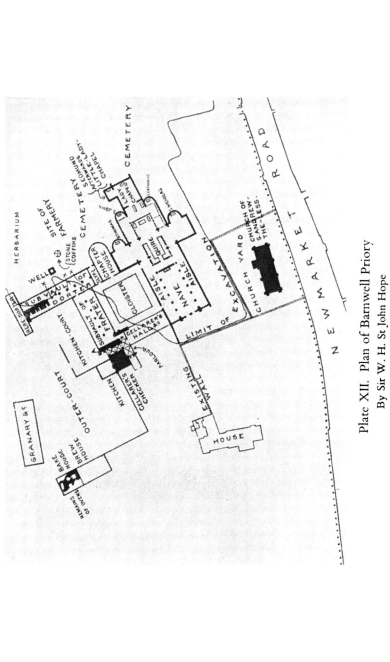

Plate XII. Plan of Barnwell Priory
By Sir W. H. St John Hope

Plate XIII. Vestiges of Barnwell Priory
From a water-colour drawing (c. 1820)   (See p. 105)

# CHAPTER IV

# BARNWELL PRIORY & THE
# OLD ABBEY HOUSE

T HE early history of the Augustinian Priory at Barnwell has fortunately been recorded in a manuscript put together from older documents probably at the end of the thirteenth century, or rather later, as it ends abruptly about 1297. It is usually called the Barnwell Cartulary, but is best described by the author's own title, *Liber Memorandorum Ecclesiae de Bernewelle*, that is, 'The Book of those things relating to the church of Barnwell which are worthy of recollection'.

This valuable document is now in the Harleian Collection in the British Museum[1]—a document closely connected with Cambridge, not only as having been drawn up in the Priory and in all probability having remained there until the dissolution of the monastery, but also in its later history.

Edward Harley, second Earl of Oxford, after whom the collection is named, and from whose widow it was acquired for the nation, was High Steward of the Borough of Cambridge[2] in the first half of the eighteenth century (1727–41). He was also for thirty years owner of the Wimpole estate in the County of Cambridge until a few

[1] MSS. Harl. 3601. Edited by J. W. Clark, 1907. The Cartulary is roughly divided into 8 vols., the last volume containing the Customs or Observances.

[2] See also 'High Stewards', Ch. II, p. 50.

months before his death when, as the result of financial difficulties, he had to part with it to Lord Chancellor Hardwicke. He had spent so much on enlarging the Hall, on his high standard of living and on his miscellaneous collections that he had run through not only his own fortune but the main part of that of his wife who had brought him Wimpole and other property as the heiress of her father John Holles, Duke of Newcastle.

Most of the manuscripts in the Harleian Collection had been accumulated by Lord Oxford's father, who might be described as a Collector of Collections. His activities as a statesman in the reign of Queen Anne may have been of a dubious character, but gratitude is due to him for his activities in preserving valuable records for posterity. Among others he had acquired the manuscripts left by Sir Simonds D'Ewes of Stow Langtoft near Lavenham in Suffolk—in 'my precious library', as Sir Simonds described it in his will. Sir Simonds was a member of St John's College, and as he specialized in unpublished monastic cartularies—or leiger-books,[1] as he called them —it is possible that he picked up the Barnwell Cartulary in Cambridge, a comparatively short time after the dissolution. This must remain as a mere supposition, but when the manuscripts of the first Earl of Oxford came into the possession of his son, the Cartulary, along with many other treasures, must have lain for years in the library at Wimpole.

[1] Sir Simonds D'Ewes, *Autobiography*, II, 99. 'Divers other manuscript cartularies or leiger-books were very lovingly lent me by Sir Edmund Bacon.' Ledger=lieger or leiger; a book that lies permanently in some place. (*New Oxford Dictionary*.)

## Barnwell Priory & the Old Abbey House

About fifty years after it had found a permanent home in the British Museum, John Nichols published a free and not very accurate translation—a paraphrase rather than a translation—of parts of the Cartulary, as one of the numbers of his *Bibliotheca Topographica*, but it was not until nearly a century later when the last remaining fragment of the Priory was presented to the Cambridge Antiquarian Society that local interest was aroused. Mr J. W. Clark then spoke of the Priory as an almost forgotten House; he set to work to collect information, and it is to him that we owe the fine edition of the Cartulary.

The story of the Priory begins at Castle End. In the reign of William Rufus there was a Baron Picot,[1] one of the companions of William of Normandy, the seat of whose barony was at Bourn, a few miles from Cambridge. Picot was High Sheriff of the County, when in 1092 his wife, the Lady Hugoline, was taken ill in Cambridge, so ill that she was given over by the King's physicians, whereupon she vowed that if she recovered her health, she would build a church in honour of St Giles, her patron saint, and also establish a religious settlement. Her husband promised to enable her to carry this out—'Upon which', adds the monkish chronicler, 'she perfectly recovered in three days'—probably aided, we should now say, by interest in her exciting plans. So Baron Picot founded the Church of St Giles, near Cambridge Castle, of which

[1] At Dives-Cabourg, near Caen, there is a little church with a tablet bearing the names of the Barons who left with William the Conqueror, including representatives of the Picot family. The name Picot is still found in Jersey and Alderney. The name of Cahaignes (Keynes) appears on the same tablet.

he had probably been made custodian by William the Conqueror, and built also a convent, where Magdalene College now stands, for six canons of the order of St Augustine brought from a monastery at Huntingdon, part of whose duty would be to serve the Church of St Giles.

Before their pious work was completed, Picot and Hugoline died, and left it in charge of their son, but he, having become involved in a conspiracy against Henry I, had to flee the country. His estates were thereupon confiscated, and granted to Pain Peverel, a famous and valiant soldier, who had been standard-bearer in the Holy Land to Robert Curthose, Duke of Normandy, brother of the King.

Peverel's father—according to Defoe—formerly called Randolph Peperking [? Peppercorn], had been a favourite of Edward the Confessor, from whom he received a 'merry grant' of Epping Forest. This grant, to quote the words of the ancient record, included rights over

> Heerte and Hind, Doe and Bocke,
> Hare and Fox, Cat (otter) and Brocke (badger),
> Wild Fowle with his Flock;
> Patrich, Pheasant Hen and Pheasant Cock,
> With Green, and wild stub and Stock.

The village of Hatfield Peverel in Essex was, therefore, Randolph Peperking's Hartfield, that is to say, Ralph Peverel's deer-park. This Ralph Peverel had a most beautiful lady to his wife, the daughter of one of Edward the Confessor's noblemen. By her he had two sons, both famous soldiers, William Peverel, Governor of Dover

Castle, and Pain Peverel, his youngest. If Defoe is correct,[1] the Peverels seem to have been one of the leading families of pre-Norman days who won the favour of the Norman kings. The name Peverel may have sounded better to Norman ears and come easier to Norman tongues than Peperking.

Be that as it may, Pain Peverel took his new responsibilities seriously and decided not only to maintain, but to enlarge, the convent which Picot had built. He wished to accommodate thirty canons, the number of his own years, but found the place too small and without the convenience of a natural spring of water. He therefore 'obtained of the King a certain place without the town of Cambridge, extending from the high-way [Newmarket Road] to the river, apparently carved out of the green, a very pleasant situation; in the midst of which piece of ground were the springs called Barnwell', or Beornwelle, the Warriors' Well,[2] so named because it was the custom for young persons to resort thither yearly on the eve of St John the Baptist, to amuse themselves with wrestling matches and other sports, a festival which gave rise to Midsummer Fair.

The canons of St Giles were moved by Pain Peverel in the year 1112 to a fine new building on this pleasant site. 'Upon this occasion', we are told, 'there was a vast concourse of clergy and laity, and of the burghers of Cam-

---

[1] Defoe, *Tour through the Eastern Counties.* Just before the appearance of *Robinson Crusoe*, it was unkindly said of Defoe in *Read's Journal* 'that the little art he is truly master of [is that] of forging a story and imposing it on the world for truth'.

[2] Reaney, *Place-names of Cambridgeshire*, p. 39. The present spelling of Barnwell occurs as early as 1268.

bridge. Their new habitation was much more commodious than their old one, and a church of wonderful beauty and solidity was begun in honour of St Giles.'

When Peverel planned the great House at Barnwell, he was acting in the spirit of the time, for the reign of Henry I was prolific in monastic institutions. The Rule of St Augustine, together with the Customs or Observances, was drawn up towards the end of the eleventh century, and between 1130 and 1135 no less than fifty-six Houses, professing the Rule of St Augustine alone, were established in this country, including the Priories of Anglesey and Barnwell.[1]

Peverel had already endowed his church with many ecclesiastical garments, very rich ornaments and 'real reliques', which he had collected in his expedition to Antioch with Robert Curthose, 'these treasures having been presented to him by the patriarch, King and nobles of that place'. In the inventory[2] taken in 1539 after the dissolution of the monastery, among the contents of the church there is mention of a 'lytell ould chest'. Two hundred years later, about the year 1740, as a labourer was digging within the priory grounds, an ancient and 'massy' wooden box, bound with iron, was discovered containing among other objects a little chest curiously ornamented with brass, $7\frac{1}{2}$ inches in length. It was divided into four compartments for the reception of consecrated treasures, the lower cell occupying the whole extent in length and being clearly appropriated for the crucifix. This reliquary

---

[1] E. Hailstone, Junior, *History and Antiquities of the Priory of Anglesey*, Camb. Antiquarian Society, 1873.

[2] The original is in the Public Record Office.

fell into the hands of Jacob Butler, then owner of the estate.[1] It is tempting to imagine that it may have been in this 'lytell ould chest' that Pain Peverel brought his relics when returning from the first Crusade.

The generous donor died too soon (in 1122) before the work was completed. His memory was perpetuated in an unusual way, for in 1275, when the canons were charged with forgetting a benefactor who had given them so many churches and so much land, 'one of them replied, "No, we can never forget him, for he sits every day at our table next the prior, and hath his portion both out of the cellar and kitchen". This, it is added, is so far true that the portion of Pain Peverel is daily set before the president in the refectory, and will be set there for ever.' It was the custom to commemorate a canon in this way for a year from the time of his death.[2]

In consequence of the final division of Peverel's estates among his four daughters, after the death of his son in the second Crusade, there was little hope of further large grants from his family, and building was delayed. Fortunately a new benefactor appeared, a famous Knight, Everard de Beche, 'a man to be respected and in all things to be commended', whose manor of Papworth[3] lay near the manor of Bourn, held by Picot, and later by Peverel,

[1] Drawings of the box are given in the Bowtell MSS. in Downing College.

[2] Marmaduke Prickett, *History of Barnwell Abbey*, p. 25. This pamphlet was based on Nichols's translation and published in aid of the fund for building the 'New Church', St Andrew the Less, at Barnwell and the Barnwell National School, in 1839.

[3] It was from Everard de Beche that the village of Upper or Over Papworth received its distinctive name of Papworth Everard.

by whom it was given to the Priory. The original plan for what was described as the 'prodigious church' begun by Peverel was, however, still found too ambitious. Part of what had already been begun was pulled down, and a 'more decent and commodious one' was built in its stead, but the choir which seems to have been completed earlier was retained. Peverel had been buried there on the north side of the High Altar; his successor, Everard de Beche, was buried in the church 'on the south side over against Pain Peverel, as the best friend of the convent next to him'.[1]

Monastic communities were governed by a Rule and also by another set of more detailed regulations due to custom only, under the title of 'Observances or Customs in accordance with the Rule', which came to be regarded as of nearly equal value with the Rule itself. The Observances in use at Barnwell were very elaborate, and were to a great extent those of the important Augustinian Abbey of St Victor at Paris.[2] These Observances have instructions for general behaviour, even including table manners, and there were special instructions, called in some monasteries the *Babees Book*, for youths who entered as novices.[3]

The following abbreviated extracts will give an idea of the domestic life of the 'brethren'. We read that in the Frater (early English name for the Refectory, the chief dining-hall) the servitors are to serve the food quickly and actively; they are to hold the dishes neither too high nor

[1] Prickett, *op. cit.* p. 13.
[2] *Customs of Augustinian Canons*, edited by J. W. Clark, pp. xxxi et seq.
[3] D. H. S. Cranage, *The Home of the Monk*, p. 24.

too low. The dishes are not to be broken, or dirty, or unsuitable, or smeared on the underside. If the servitor cannot bring the brethren all they ask for, he ought nevertheless to reply to them civilly. The brethren ought all to be careful not to wipe their noses, or rub their teeth, on the napkins or tablecloths, or cut them with their knives.

The Sub-Cellarer, or store-keeper, should be obliging and of a cheerful countenance, and when he has no substance to distribute may hand out a gentle reply, for a soft answer turneth away wrath.

The Chamberlain is to provide a laundress of good character. She must be able properly to wash and mend all the linen of the brethren, namely, surplices, rochets, sheets, shirts, and drawers. If any articles are missing through the carelessness of the laundress, she is herself to make them good out of her wages.

The Hosteller, or Keeper of the Guest House, is to show cheerful hospitality. It is part of his duty to keep clean cloths and clean towels; cups without flaws; spoons of silver; mattresses, blankets, sheets not merely clean but untorn; proper pillows, quilts to cover the beds, and of right size and pleasing colour; fires that do not smoke. The whole Guest House is to be kept clear of spiders' webs and dirt, and—here after requirements suitable at the present day we are suddenly transported to medieval times—the rooms are to be strewn with rushes underfoot, with a sufficient quantity of straw in the beds. (Dr Ennion, in his book *Adventurers Fen*, mentions that a special kind of sedge, sweet flag, was used to straw the floors of monasteries and priories.) A more modern touch is given again as we read that there are to be keys and locks to the doors, and good bolts on the inside, so as to keep the doors securely closed while the guests are asleep.

The conditions in the Guest House were clearly important, as the Priory had many royal and distinguished visitors. King John stayed there in 1200; Lord Hugh, Bishop of Ely, held full synod there in 1236; Henry III paid a visit in 1258; Edward I's chancellor resided there in 1293 while the King was housed in the Castle. The Chancellor had charge of the King's treasure-chest containing £1000 which was deposited in the Priory, and fifty of the royal horses had to be accommodated. As a parting present, King Edward gave gold altar-cloths for the High Altar. In 1295 two papal legates arrived as visitors. In 1325 Edward II spent several days at the Priory, and in the following year his wife, Queen Isabella, also stayed there when conspiring against her husband. In 1388 the young King, Richard II, in the middle of his troublous reign, not only made it his headquarters, but summoned Parliament to meet him at the Priory. In the fifteenth and sixteenth centuries it was frequently the meeting-place for Synods of the Diocese, and Judges of Assize usually lodged there. Thorney, a mitred abbey, and Barnwell Priory were the only two 'greater' monasteries, as they were called, in Cambridgeshire. Hence the Abbot and the Prior were the highest in ecclesiastical rank after the Bishop of Ely.

Litigation was incessant; records of law-suits, in the technical language of the lawyers of the thirteenth century, are intermingled in the Cartulary with anecdotes in colloquial Latin. These legal proceedings refer to a great variety of matters; sometimes it is a question of the ownership of land or of rents, for the Prior, as representing the Priory, was a large landowner; or he may have to answer to the King for an infringement of royal rights. There were also repeated disputes between the canons of Barnwell and the burgesses of Cambridge, and between the Priory and the University—and so on. F. W. Maitland wrote an Introduction to J. W. Clark's edition of the *Liber Memorandorum*, consisting of twenty pages of notes on the legal matters mentioned in the period covered, that is, from 1112 to 1297. In summing up, Maitland remarked that owing to the preservation of this manuscript we have a singularly good opportunity of investigating the temporal and economic side of the history of a religious house. 'I do not know', he said, 'of any monastic book which displays so many and such various entries from judicial records.'

With the building and rebuilding, which went on for many years, with the administration of the large establishment and the affairs of the numerous manors and advowsons with which the monastery was endowed, the Priors must have had their hands full. The first Prior, Geoffrey who had come with the canons from Huntingdon to St Giles and thence to Barnwell, presided altogether for twenty years and having seen the brethren established in their new home 'died at a very great age'. Prior Gerard, his successor, is described as a very cheerful and merry companion, whereby he was recommended to the good liking of his patron, Pain Peverel.

Some of the Priors are little more than names and the list is not complete, but in 1255 we make the acquaintance of Prior Jolan de Thorleye, who is described as 'a very little man, but of a very commendable understanding, and well versed in the civil law'—an important qualification in such litigious times.

Jolan made great efforts to restore the revenues of the Priory, which had been declining,[1] and had so far succeeded that he was enabled to increase the number of canons to thirty, as originally intended. He was also progressing with the buildings when the Barons' Wars broke out in 1263. The Bishop of Ely and Prior Jolan were of the King's party, but the Bishop failed in defending the Isle of Ely, which surrendered to Simon de Montfort and became the stronghold of rebellion. The loyal Prior Jolan was not left unmolested, and when travelling in Norfolk was robbed of thirteen good horses and all his equipment, while his retinue was put to flight and he himself made an ignominious retreat to Dereham Abbey. Not long afterwards, the Prior's Manor at Bourn was plundered and burnt, and the Priory itself attacked. One day, a certain fellow of prodigious stature, called Philip le Champion, came and pulled the diminutive Prior out of bed at dawn, and demanded the surrender of all his stores. Friends of the Prior came to the rescue, there was a general drawing of swords, and a serious conflict was with difficulty avoided. The King, Henry III, thought it time to intervene; Cambridge was made his headquarters, forti-

[1] Twenty years earlier, in 1235, a bond had been drawn up between the Prior and Convent of Barnwell and the Italian merchants, called Caursini, agents of the Pope, who are said to have been even more usurious than the Jews of those days. The bond, for a large sum at extortionate interest, is given at length in Tovey's *Anglia-Judaica*, ed. 1738, and is quoted by Prickett, *op. cit.* p. 17.

fications were begun, and his brother Richard, styled King of the Romans, or alternatively of Alemaine, was lodged in the Priory. When the King had to return hastily in order to defend London, the defence of Cambridge collapsed, and malcontent soldiers returning in disorder to the Isle 'debated whether they should burn down all the priory, but especially the hall where the King of Almain lodged'.[1]

The situation was saved only by the intervention of members of the Peche family,[2] to whom the patronage of the Priory had passed by the marriage of an ancestor of theirs to a daughter of Pain Peverel. Sir Hugh Peche and his brother protested that they would sooner die than suffer the bones of their father and ancestors, who were buried in the church, to be burnt. They carried the day, against the wish of many of their party.

Under these disturbances and other afflictions, Prior Jolan broke down in health and resigned. After a time he was able to return to Barnwell and, although no longer Prior, was allowed to superintend the architectural improvements that were in progress at the time of his resignation. He was allowed to build a handsome room for himself and was granted a pension which he enjoyed for sixteen years, but an official visit by the Archbishop of Canterbury unfortunately upset this happy arrangement and a room was assigned to him in the Farmery (Infirmary), where he died two years later. He would be well tended there, for in accordance with the Observances

[1] Prickett, *op. cit.* p. 21.
[2] The name 'Peche' is also spelt 'Pecché', and is probably the same as Peachey, a name still found in Cambridgeshire.

of the Monastery, the Master of the Farmery had instructions that he ought frequently to take note of the condition of the sick; he should ask them, with kindly interest, whether they wish for anything; and bestow on them all the consolation in his power. Further he should provide, in a spirit of fraternal sympathy, a fire on the hearth, should the state of the weather require it, a candle, a cresset, and a lamp to burn all night, and everything that is necessary, useful and proper.

Periodic bleeding was practised as a matter of routine, and three classes of the sick were recognized. There were brethren who sometimes fell into a state of weak health from the irksomeness of life in the Cloister, or from long continuance of silence; sometimes from fatigue in singing or extension of fasting; sometimes from sleeplessness or overwork; while some were afflicted with a sense of heaviness in the head, and pain in the stomach from sitting up too late with guests, and either drinking too much, or overloading the stomach with food. Some, on the other hand, if severely punished were so much disturbed in spirit, that they moved about among their fellows as though they were half dead. Such did not require medicine, but only repose and comforts; they might walk in the vineyard,[1] the garden, and along the riverside, or even into the fields, and woods. They might absent themselves, for a short time, from the Quire, from study, and

[1] William of Malmesbury, writing early in the twelfth century, when describing the grounds of Thorney Abbey, also in Cambridgeshire, mentioned 'a field overspread with vines, either creeping upon the ground or climbing up poles to support them'. It has been said that members of many religious Houses, who came from France, planted vineyards, but found them unsuccessful in the climate of this island.

from the Cloister, and so, by repose, diet, and recreation, regain before long their former state of health.[1]

Another class of sick persons suffered from attacks of fever, tertian or quotidian; intolerable toothaches; sharp gouty spasms; affections of the eyes, the throat, the liver, and pains in divers parts of the body. The Warden of the Order, pitying them like a mother, would kindly give them leave to enter the Farmery. The Master of the Farmery ought to consult a physician, and provide them with baths, draughts, electuaries, and all other things conducive to a speedy convalescence.

A third class of sick persons included some who were struck with illness so suddenly that they lost the strength of their limbs in an instant. Those near the person taken ill ought at once to carry him into the Farmery. The Master of the Farmery should always be at hand that the patient should want for nothing to relieve his infirmity or his suffering, for no book or chalice ought to be considered too precious to be given for the life of a brother in this extremity.

If all these customs were religiously followed, the Farmery would indeed be a well-managed hospital.

Although peace had been restored, Jolan's successor, Symon de Ascellis, one of the canons of Barnwell, was not without his trials. Soon after the battle of Evesham in 1265, William of St Omer, the King's Justiciary, took up residence in the Priory, while he was inquiring into the state of things in the Isle of Ely, one of the last places to hold out against the King. He stayed a whole year,

---

[1] Dr D. H. S. Cranage, in *The Home of the Monk*, says there is no doubt that the tedium of the life was often found to be insupportable.

with a great retinue, and also his wife, who would sometimes have twenty-two female attendants—surely very
upsetting for the routine and resources of the monastery.

Then in 1276, a quarrel having occurred between one
of the Canons and a scholar of the University, the Chancellor of the University summoned the Canon to answer
the charge. The Canon refused to obey and was promptly
excommunicated by the Chancellor. Much altercation
ensued, but the matter was finally settled by the Bishop
of Ely,[1] who declared the monks of Barnwell to be entirely
exempt from the authority of the Chancellor of the
University. The Chancellor's successor, Roger de Ful-
bourn, became later a generous benefactor to the Priory.

By the end of the thirteenth century, the monasteries
were diminishing in popular esteem in consequence of
various abuses, and support was largely transferred to the
Friars. Some lands and livings, however, still continued
to fall to the Priory as is illustrated by an entry in the
Calendar of Patent Rolls 1361-4 (p. 190) showing that
in 1362 Thomas de Elteslee, rector of Grantchester, and
his brother, Alan de Elteslee, rector of Lolworth,[2] had
licence to give in mortmain lands, etc. to the Prior and
Convent of Barnwell.

In 1287, Symon still being Prior, a dreadful accident
had befallen the Church of the Priory. On 3 February,
St Blaise's day (Prickett calls the Bishop, St Blaze), the
Cross on the top of the tower was set on fire by a terrible

---

[1] The Bishopric of Ely was founded in 1107, only five years earlier
than Barnwell Priory.

[2] A list of rectors in Lolworth Church gives the name as Alan
Banestre.

flash of lightning; the sparks that fell from it were 'like apples of gold'. The burning Cross itself finally fell on the Choir and set fire to it, doing incredible damage, which took over a year to repair. Another account adds that a great part of the domestic buildings of the monastery were also destroyed, and other houses at a distance set on fire by the sparks from the Cross.

After all these disasters, the fortunes of the Priory seem to have run more smoothly (subject only to almost continuous litigation), and a century later an outstanding event was the meeting of Parliament summoned by Richard II which occupied the Priory from 10 September to 17 October 1388. The roll of this Parliament—known as the Cambridge Parliament—is not forthcoming, but its work has left its mark on the Statute Book and was carefully recorded by a chronicler, called the Monk of Westminster.[1] The identity of the Monk of Westminster was fully discussed by Dr Armitage Robinson, the Dean of Westminster, in a paper read to the British Academy in 1907. The monk has usually been assumed to be John of Malvern, who continued Higden's Polychronicon to 1381, but he was never a monk of Westminster, as his name does not appear on the Chamberlain's Rolls. Dr Robinson's purpose was to claim the portion of the Chronicle 1381–94 (discovered in a MS. of Corpus Christi College, Cambridge) for a monk of Westminster who chronicled the events of his own time. His conclusion was that the evidence was on the side of John Lakyngheth, clearly a person of first-rate importance in the Abbey from 1362 to 1392, when he retired. He died in 1396.

[1] Tout, *Mediæval History*, III, 440.

Whether he 'devoted his few years of leisure to the continuation of John Malvern's work we shall perhaps never know', adds Dr Robinson, but a native of Lakenheath, a village only a few miles from Mildenhall, might well have taken special interest in such an important local event as the Cambridge Parliament of 1388.

Fuller's comments are characteristic:[1]

A parliament was called at Cambridge; a place at this time very convenient for that purpose. For he that will hinder the hide from rising up on either side, must fix his foot on the middle thereof. Cambridge was well nigh the center of those eastern counties, lately mutinous with popular commotions. The king for his privacy was pleased to prefer Barnwell Priory for the place of his repose, though otherwise King's Hall (founded by his Grandfather), was prepared for his entertainment; where all things were so conveniently contrived, that the courtiers had all lodgings and offices by themselves, without meeting with the Scholars, save only in the passage towards the kitchen. ...

By the way, methinks Cambridge might bring an action of trespass against all our printed statute-books, for depriving her of the honour of this parliament, and rendering the place Canterbury instead of Cambridge, in the preface to the acts thereof. This inconvenience cometh from contracting long words in writing, when there be two names whose faces, (as I may say) I mean their beginnings, are the same; and whose lower parts, though much differing, being cut off with a dash, causeth confusion betwixt them. ...The best is, it matters not where good statutes be made, so they be made; the place not being essential unto them.

[1] Dr Thomas Fuller (1608–61), *History of the University of Cambridge* (ed. Prickett and Wright), pp. 119–21.

## Barnwell Priory & the Old Abbey House

Many and good were the laws enacted in this parliament, besides the confirmation of those made in the reign of King Edward the Third, viz. That the manly and martial exercise of archery should be generally used. Secondly, a statute was made against the multitude of servants, great lords keeping then little armies in their families, which soon after occasioned the wars betwixt the houses of York and Lancaster. And whereas it was the general complaint, that men were grown so vain and expensive in their clothes, that servants were not to be known from their masters, the clergy from the laiety, something was ordered for the regulating of apparel, the wages of labourers,[1] and removing the staple.

The removal of the Staple mentioned by Fuller marks one more stage in a vacillating policy with regard to its location. The 'Staple' (late M.E. emporium, mart), a place appointed by royal authority

where English goods for export had to be collected, taxed and sold, was necessary for levying the customs on which the King's finances depended.... At one time it was fixed in certain English towns, then in Flanders [at Middelburg], finally in Calais, which English arms won [in 1347] and held as the port of entry into France.[2]

The famous siege of Calais which had lasted for a year ended in the dramatic scene when Queen Philippa on her knees won from her husband, Edward III, pardon for the self-sacrificing burghers of Calais. Edward then planted

[1] What Fuller describes as regulating the wages of labourers was a re-enactment of the Statute of Labourers with new safeguards for binding the labourer to his native village—a reactionary movement due to the Peasants' rising of 1381.

[2] Trevelyan, *Social History*, p. 34.

( 99 )

an English colony there, and in 1362 established the first Staple in Calais.

The class of goods dealt with by the Staple consisted mainly of wool, and Calais, with partial alterations from time to time, seems to have held the Staple for two hundred years from the date of the Cambridge Parliament, until the loss of Calais in 1588, shortly before the death of Mary Tudor. By that time, the conditions of trade were changing, export of wool was giving place to woollen cloth, and in Elizabeth's reign 'our merchants found new and more distant markets, some of them on the other side of the globe, in place of that commerce with the Netherlands and France, which had from time immemorial furnished the principal vent of English goods'.[1]

About ten years later, a poem, written when Richard was deposed but still living, exhorts him to repent and shows how extravagant expenditure had compelled him to summon a parliament.

Neither fines, forfeitures, fee-farms, wardships, profits of the law courts, revenues of the crown lands, nor the wool customs were sufficient, says the poet, for the upkeep of Richard's household, without his applying to a parliament for a grant of tonnage and poundage and for a tenth and fifteenth. The money bags were empty and had to be refilled.[2]

From the reign of Richard II until the reign of Henry VII, records of the Priory are scanty, but in 1504 we come across a substantial endowment on the part of a certain Richard King, of Wisbech.

[1] Trevelyan, *Social History*, p. 192.
[2] Dr Helen Cam, *Liberties and Communities in Medieval England*, p. 229.

He gave to the Prior and Convent of Barnwell the Falcon in Petty Cury in Cambridge; a waste place called the Plough, lying towards the gate of the Friars Preachers;[1] a tenement with a dove-house and garden adjoining, abutting upon the Friars Preachers lane; and 28 acres of arable land in the fields of Cambridge and Barnwell.[2]

Elaborate instructions were given for a requiem, a dirge, and a solemn Mass, with gratuities to those officiating, and a distribution to every person present of

a halfpenny loaf and two herrings, as far as ten shillings would go. The Master of Michael House or a fellow deputed by him, was to oversee these exequies, and to have 2s. with his breakfast at the Prior's table, and for his servant with the Prior's servant.

In the following year, 1505, there were for the last time great disputes between the Corporation and the Prior and Convent of Barnwell. Conflicting claims were made to the right of fishing in that part of the river adjoining the manor of Chesterton, of which the Prior and Convent were lords. In the course of these disputes, John Bell, Mayor of the town, 1564-5, and the Prior came to blows, and 'laid violent hands on one another', as reported in the Corporation Muniments. Their differences were at length referred to arbitrators, who in the course of a long and careful award, decreed that the mayor, burgesses, and their successors for ever were to have uninterrupted liberty of fishing and fowling in the stream from Nun's lake

[1] Friars Preachers, or Dominicans, occupied the present site of Emmanuel College.

[2] Nichols, *History and Antiquities of Barnwell Abbey*, pp. 71-4. Quoted by Cooper, *Annals of Cambridge*, 1, 273.

[St Rhadegund's] to the stone wall of the west part of the House of Barnwell. Also that the Prior and Convent of Barnwell and their successors for evermore should have all liberty of fishing and fowling in Barnwell pool, and from the Old Ferry at Chesterton to Ditton lake. Both parties were to undertake to forgive all controversies and trespasses from the beginning of the world until the day of the agreement.[1]

The relations between Barnwell Priory and the neighbouring Priory of Anglesey, both of the Augustinian Order, must have been intimate. Their lands in the Open Fields of Cambridge met at several points, and there were meetings of the officials for ecclesiastical and other purposes. It is recorded, for instance, that in 1461, when Thomas Norton was appointed to the episcopal throne of Ely—the same Bishop who took a leading part in the attempt to drain the fens, and gave his name to a cut, called 'Norton's leam'—great festivities were held in Ely at his installation. The Abbots of Thorney, Bury and Ramsey, and the Priors of Ely, Barnwell and Anglesey were present and were invited to a sumptuous dinner after the ceremony. All kinds of fish, flesh and fowl that the fen-country could produce were served at the feast, while between the courses appropriate verses were sung by the minstrels in readiness.[2] Definite proof of cordial feeling occurred in 1515, when William Seggewyke of Reche, a Canon of Barnwell, was elected as Prior of Anglesey. Some hesitation was shown by Seggewyke, possibly on account of the circumstances attending the retirement of the former Prior, who had held office for a

[1] Corporation Cross Book, p. 79.    [2] Hailstone, *op. cit.* p. 300.

very short time and appears to have been displaced by order of Queen Catherine, wife of Henry VIII. Segge-wyke's scruples were, however, overcome, and his election was confirmed after the resignation of the retiring prior had been received by Master William Fayrhayr, doctor of laws, representing the Archbishop of Canter-bury.[1]

But the end was approaching for both these Houses. The Act for the annexation to the Crown of certain smaller monasteries, of which Anglesey was one, had been passed between January 1535 and February 1536. In 1539 Barnwell Priory with all its revenues had to be surrendered to Henry VIII among sixty of the Greater Houses suppressed between 1538 and 1540.

The closing passage of the Rule of St Augustine runs as follows:

Even as a lofty tower, surrounded on all sides by walls, makes the soldiers who garrison it safe, fearless and impregnable, so the Rule of blessed Augustine, fortified on all sides by Observances in accordance with it, makes its soldiers, that is Canons regular, undismayed at the attacks of devils, safe and invincible.

They might defy devils, but were helpless before the civil power.

After the dissolution, not only the contents of the buildings at Barnwell were sold, but roof-tiles, floors, windows, glass, and iron, as set out in the inventory of 1538. The site was granted to Lord Clinton, and other private owners followed, including Dr Thomas Wendy of

[1] *Ibid.* pp. 302–8.

Haslingfield, 'the doyen of the medical profession', physician to four successive monarchs, including Henry VIII, and one of the witnesses of his Will. Wendy's son, who died in 1559, is said to have given more than 182 loads of stone from the Priory towards the rebuilding of the Chapel of Bene't College, now Corpus Christi. The Priory must therefore have fallen into a ruinous condition by that time. The estate was afterwards held by the Chicheley family, of Arrington and Wimpole, and in 1659 Alexander Butler obtained it in exchange for an estate at Orwell from Sir Thomas Chicheley, father of another Sir Thomas who became High Steward of the Borough in 1670.[1] Alexander Butler 'then came hither to dwell, being the first owner that lived thereon since the dissolution'. It is not known when the present house was built—probably about 1660; the date 1678 placed by Ambrose Butler on the gable, twenty years after his father had taken possession, must refer to an addition to the house. The Butler family retained possession for a hundred years, until the death in 1765 of Jacob Butler, grandson of Alexander, an eccentric character, known as Squire Butler.

In Alexander Butler's time, it was his custom, as Alderman Newton mentions in his *Diary*, to entertain the Mayor and Aldermen, in connexion with Midsummer Fair. The Alderman describes their visit in 1669:

The Mayor in his Gowne with Marsh the Serjeant in his Gowne and with the mace, before the Mayer, the Aldermen and rest in their Cloakes went to Barnewell Abbey to M<sup>r</sup>

---

[1] See also 'High Stewards', Ch. II, p. 46.

Butlers....There at M^r Butlers charge all the company had Gamon of Bacon, creame and stewed pruens and strong beere and cake the Towne sent wine and sugar and soe after the Treat done the Company went away from thence....Then we went to the mayors booth in Midsomer fayre and dranke some cans of beere...and from thence went home accompanying the Mayor...nothing but a tankard of small beere at M^r Mayors before we went from thence.[1]

During the century when the Butlers held the estate, the ruins of the Priory seem to have been spared by them and for fifty years afterwards, but after Lord Gwydir came into possession of the property in 1809, the remains of the monastery were rapidly destroyed for the sake of the stone which was very scarce in the district. Bowtell (whose papers are preserved in Downing College) writes that in

the years 1810–12 when the foundations of this ancient fabric were dug up, and part of the remaining walls pulled down for building materials, the whole site of the priory was covered with fragments of octagonal stone pillars, of various dimensions, and slender round columns of purbeck marble, mingled with capitals, and other architectural ornaments which had decorated the building of this spacious monastery.

Bowtell adds that in 1810, enough was left to prove it a work of great magnitude, and vestiges of ancient magnificence were then traceable in sundry parts of its walls.

Lord Gwydir inherited the Barnwell property through his wife, a descendant of the Pantons, a family well known in Newmarket. Thomas Panton, Chief Groom, or Equerry,

[1] *Diary of Samuel Newton,* Alderman of Cambridge (1662–1717), p. 48, edited by J. E. Foster, for the Cambridge Antiquarian Society, 1890.

to George II, and master of the King's 'running-horses', bought *c.* 1769 land all round Fen Ditton—he lived in Ditton Hall. His purchases included Sturbridge Fair Ground, the Leper Chapel, the Priory site, and probably the intervening lands. His daughter married the Duke of Ancaster, a title now extinct. His son, another Thomas, was like his father a lover of horses; he kept race-horses, was an early member of the Jockey Club and won the Derby in 1786. He was anxious to enclose the open fields of Barnwell,[1] but was opposed by the University, who thought their rides would be curtailed, and consequently their health injured, if they could no longer gallop over the open fields adjoining Cambridge.[2] In 1807 the bill for authorizing the enclosure was carried through the House of Commons in spite of the opposition from the University. 'In the House of Lords it was still opposed by some of the Colleges who had contrived to get Lord Thurlow on their side. The learned Lord had actually risen to oppose it, when some person sitting near him called out loud enough to be heard by my informant— "This is the bill of your old friend, Tommy Panton!"— (for so he was called to the day of his death). The noble lord immediately resumed his seat, and did not utter another syllable.'[3] The Bill received the royal assent in the same year.

As 'Tommy' Panton left no heir, his lands including

[1] The open fields on the eastern side of Cambridge may have been named after the Priory which owned about one-third.

[2] A delightful picture of ladies and gentlemen enjoying this exercise can be seen in Loggan's print of the eastern fields.

[3] Gunning, *Reminiscences of Cambridge*, II, 39, 40.

the Barnwell Priory estate went to his niece, Lady Gwydir, daughter of the Duchess of Ancaster. In 1820 the whole property passed to Lady Gwydir's son, who sold it in lots to various persons—Fen Ditton, including Barnwell, was bought by Dr Haviland, a Cambridge physician.

The Barnwell property subsequently changed hands several times. The Abbey House found tenants, but the main part of the site remained practically unused and uncultivated. In the year 1886 some excavations were attempted, but the ground had been dug over so thoroughly in 1812 that it was impossible to trace with any certainty the foundations of the buildings and little of interest was found.

The estate had been bought in 1879 by Mr Joseph Sturton, who made roads and sold most of the land in small building plots. Fortunately, enough was enclosed to form a garden for the Abbey House. The only remnant of the Priory buildings, standing on a small plot of ground near the garden was given by Mr Sturton to the Cambridge Antiquarian Society.

Mr T. D. Atkinson, then practising in Cambridge as an architect, drew up a detailed report on the structure as it was at that time. After careful examination he was of opinion that it formed part of a living-room where refinement and comfort were considered, its fire-place, its windows with seats in the recesses and the highly finished masonry supporting this view, although it has usually been called the Cellarer's checker or office.

Can this have been the 'handsome room' built by Jolan for his own use?

For many years the old Abbey House was divided into

three parts, the latest owner being Mr Thomas Askham, who occupied the central portion. In 1945 the freehold was bought from Mr Askham by Lord Fairhaven of Anglesey Abbey and presented by him to the Cambridge and County Folk Museum, the house to be reunited and together with the grounds used for the benefit of the community, as an expression of thanksgiving for the preservation of the nation in the recent perils.

The original Folk Museum, now outgrown, is at Castle End, opposite the modern church that has replaced Picot's Church of St Giles. Thus, more than eight centuries after the historic migration of the Canons of St Giles from Castle End to Barnwell, another migration is to take place—again to Barnwell from Castle End.

CHAPTER V

# WHY OXFORD COMES FIRST

## A PROBLEM IN PRECEDENCE

A CAMBRIDGE PROFESSOR,[1] addressing an Oxford audience, once wittily remarked that the oldest of all Inter-University Sports was a Lying Match. Oxford claimed that it was founded by Mempricius in the days of Samuel the Prophet, and Cambridge retaliated by dating its origin from the Spanish Cantaber[2] in the days of Gurguntius Brabtruc.

The scarce sources of information on the origin of the two ancient Universities certainly left a wide field for fable and imagination, and heated controversy took place from time to time. Ingulph, Abbot of Croyland in East Anglia in the eleventh century, Secretary to William of Normandy, and Peter of Blois, Archdeacon of Bath in the twelfth century, Secretary to Queen Eleanor, Mother of Richard Cœur de Lion, were long regarded as the leading authorities on this subject, but the writings attributed to them have not been able to stand the test of modern research and are now regarded as spurious.

Notwithstanding much research, however, authentic information still remains scanty. The probability is that both Universities arose towards the end of the twelfth century, a time when many men of scholarly tastes were

[1] F. W. Maitland, Downing Professor of English Law, 1888–1907.
[2] 270 B.C.

( 109 )

conscious of their ignorance of developments taking place in theology and canon law. Schools to meet their needs were formed in Cambridge and Oxford and became permanent.[1] The earliest Cambridge students would naturally come from the Fenland Monasteries at Anglesey, Ely, Ramsey and Croyland. The University of Paris, which served as a model for both Oxford and Cambridge, took form in the first half of the twelfth century, Oxford probably between 1150 and 1180, Cambridge certainly before 1209, possibly between 1180 and 1190. Our University history would therefore seem to date from the commencement of our true national history, from the time when Norman and Saxon had become fused, when the invader had been driven from our shores, and the national character began to assume its distinctive form.[2]

But through the long period before this slight amount of firm ground had been attained, tradition based on fable held the field, and from time to time, especially during the sixteenth and seventeenth centuries, the contest described by Maitland was carried on with considerable warmth in both camps.

Among the young students whom Eton had sent up to King's College early in the sixteenth century was one Richard Croke, a youth of good family and promising talents. After having taken his bachelor's degree he went to Oxford to study Greek under Grocyn, and from there to the Continent, where he taught in several Universities with conspicuous success, while his patron and friend Erasmus was teaching at Cambridge. After seven years'

[1] W. W. Rouse Ball, *Cambridge Papers*, pp. 180 *et seq.*
[2] J. B. Mullinger, *University of Cambridge*, p. 84.

absence he returned to his own University, and in 1519 was appointed Reader in Greek. In his inaugural oration[1] he warned Cambridge that the Oxford men, whom up to the present time they had outstripped in every department of knowledge, were betaking themselves to Greek in good earnest, and added that the Oxonians had solicited him with the offer of a handsome salary. 'But', he said, 'feelings of respectful loyalty towards this University— and especially towards that most noble society of scholars, King's College, to which I owe my first acquirements in the art of eloquence—have enjoined that I should first offer my services to you.'

Shortly afterwards Croke delivered another oration, less interesting than the first, but containing one note-worthy and contentious passage in which he spoke of Oxford as *colonia a Cantabrigia deducta,* again exhorting the University not to allow itself to be outstripped by those who were once its disciples.[2]

On another occasion Cambridge attempted to score a point in the contest when in 1564, Queen Elizabeth paid her famous visit to the University.[3] Coming to Cambridge from Haslingfield on horseback, the Queen entered by way of King's College, 'dressed in a gown of black velvet pinked: a call upon her head set with pearls and pretious stones; a hat that was spangled with gold, and a bush of feathers'. Having arrived at the west door of the Chapel, and hearing that the Orator would with her permission speak for the University, she inquired for him and willed him to begin. William Masters, Fellow of

[1] Mullinger, *op. cit.* pp. 534–5.   [2] *Ibid.* p. 539.
[3] See also 'Cambridge Waits', Ch. III, p. 71.

King's College, and Public Orator, then made his oration, of length almost half an hour. A translation of the speech, which was in Latin, is given in a narrative by Dr Nicholas Robynson, Bishop of Bangor.[1] In the course of the oration, Masters described the antiquity of the University and claimed—as quoted by Maitland—that Cambridge had been established by Cantaber, and that it is 'much older than Oxford or Paris; and out of the which, as out of a most clear fountain, they sprang'.[2]

The Queen commended him for his oration, and 'much marvelled that his memory did so well serve him, repeating such divers and sundry matters'. His 'inconsiderate boast', however, opened anew the flood-gates of controversy, and was 'really like a letting out of waters', for in the dispute that ensued, three hundred and eighty writers were said to have been on the side of Oxford, and one hundred and ten on that of Cambridge.[3]

Dr Caius, Master of Gonville Hall, afterwards Gonville and Caius College, continued the controversy in 1568, and other antiquaries carried on the fray after his time. One of them, Brian Twyne,[4] Fellow of Corpus Christi College, Oxford, went so far as to suggest that Croke's *Colonia* mentioned in his oration a century earlier, was really nothing but the 'Trojan' party in Oxford, a reactionary

[1] This narrative is given in Nichols, *Progresses of Queen Elizabeth*, vol. III.

[2] From a narrative by Matthew Stokys, Fellow of King's, one of the Esquire Bedells, and Registrary of the University 1558–91. Quoted by Cooper in *Annals of Cambridge*, II, 189 et seq.

[3] Rev. J. J. Smith, *The Cambridge Portfolio*, 1840, I, 159–60.

[4] Twyne is said to have been largely responsible for the Oxford Statutes drawn up at that time.

party of young students said to have come from Cambridge, who objected to the study of Greek in 1519 about the time of Croke's oration.[1] This 'venomous suggestion' enraged Dr Thomas Fuller, of Queens' College, Cambridge, who charged Twyne with 'buzzing jealousies into the heads of the readers, to shake the credit of such authors who write anything in the honour of Cambridge'— dealing with him 'the more mildly', as he said, 'because he is (and I know not how soon I may be) dead'.[2] Anthony Wood, of Merton College, Oxford, a contemporary of Fuller, defended Twyne, his ire having been specially stirred by Croke's allusion to Oxford as a colony from Cambridge—an allusion never forgiven and never forgotten. Fuller himself expressed the view that it was unnecessary to make 'odious comparisons', or to 'regulate the pre-eminence of our English Universities'. The matter was not, however, allowed to rest there, and four times in the seventeenth century—three of them in Fuller's lifetime—the question of precedence was debated in Parliament, each time as a side issue.

On the first occasion, in 1605, the Bill under discussion was for the purpose of prohibiting the residence of married men with their wives and families in Colleges and Halls of Cambridge and Oxford. In the report stage, it was noticed that the 'clerk's man', accustomed no doubt to alphabetical order, had put Cambridge before Oxford, and there was 'a great Dispute, and much Time spent in the House: And at last it came to Question, Whether Cambridge, or Oxford, first: And Resolved, with much

[1] Mullinger, *op. cit.* p. 539.     [2] Fuller, *op. cit.* p. 33.

Odds, that Oxford.' The Bill in that form was passed by the Commons, but afterwards thrown out by the Lords, so the burning question was still undecided.

In 1621 the matter again arose in the Lords on a Bill of Subsidy, in which Oxford was named before Cambridge. 'It was much debated amongst the Lords what course may be taken for an equality between the said two Universities, that the one might not have precedence of the other; but nothing concluded herein.' Further information was required, and the problem was shelved until the antiquity of the two Universities could be proved. An investigation and report were ordered, but there is no record that any report was ever received.

Twenty years later, in 1640, in another Bill of Subsidy for the King's Army, Cambridge was once more placed before Oxford in a proviso exempting the Universities.[1] The Bill was

disputed and debated in a Grand Committee; and when it came to the clause where Cambridge was placed before Oxford, many of the House that had been Oxford-Men, cried to have Oxford first; but the Cambridge-Men cried, that the Bill should stand as it was; and thereupon the Oxford-Men called to have it put to the question; and divers Cambridge-Men called upon Sir Simonds D'Ewes.[2]

Now, Sir Simonds, who lived near Lavenham and had just been elected to Parliament for Sudbury in Suffolk, was a member of St John's College, Cambridge, and a

[1] Exemption had been originally granted by Elizabeth in 1561. See p. 40.
[2] Cooper, *op. cit.* III, 307-9.

writer on antiquarian subjects.[1] He pleaded that they should dispute it by reason and not make an 'idol of either place'.

If [he said] I do not prove that Cambridge was a renown'd City at least 500 Years before there was a House in Oxford standing, and whilst Brute Beasts fed, and Corn was sown on that Place where that City is now seated: And that Cambridge was a Nursery of Learning before Oxford was known to have a Grammar-School in it, I will yield up the Bucklers.

If [Sir Simonds continued] I should spend time to reckon up the vain Allegations produced for the Antiquity of Oxford, by Twyne; and of Cambridge, by Caius, I should but repeat the Dreams of the Antients; for I account the most they have published in Print to be no better. But I find, by Authority without Exception, that in the antient Catalogue of the British Cities, Cambridge is the ninth in Number, where London itself is but the eleventh. And who would have thought that Oxford would have contended for Precedency with Cambridge, which London gave it 1200 years since.

After basing his theory on various documents which later research has included in the *Dreams of the Antients*, Sir Simonds concludes: 'And so I have done with Cambridge as a renown'd Place.' He then proceeds:

And now I come to speak of it as it hath been a Nursery of Learning:...it grew so famous for Learning about the time of William I the Norman, that he sent his younger son Henry thither, to be there instructed; who was afterwards King of

[1] D'Ewes was also the author of *Journals of all the Parliaments during the reign of Elizabeth. Winthrop Papers*, 1638–44, vol. IV, contains letters from Winthrop to Sir Simonds D'Ewes of Lavenham. Massachusett's Historical Society, 1945.

England by the name of Henry I, and was surnamed Beau-clerke, in respect of his great and uncommon Knowledge.

Having thus established to his own satisfaction that Cambridge was in all respects the elder Sister, Sir Simonds' advice finally was that the present Bill should pass as it was penned;[1] to avoid division among themselves as well as to entomb all further emulation and the rather because Oxford had the precedence in the last Bill of the same nature that passed the House.[2] In the Bill, therefore, as adopted, Oxford was placed before Cambridge.

But even this decision was not final, for in 1660, when a Bill was introduced for establishing a General Letter Office, and a proviso was introduced for making special arrangements for the Universities, a great debate arose as to whether Oxford should be put before Cambridge. One speaker objected to 'making a variance between two Sisters, by making them quarrel, like women, about place'. Another pointed out 'that if the proviso passed as it was, it would shew that Oxford men could fast better than Cambridge, because he observed that many of the others were gone to dinner'. The House finally avoided the difficulty by passing the proviso in a form in which neither Oxford nor Cambridge was named. They were merely 'the two Universities'.[3]

In recent times, Rashdall,[4] in his great work on the *Universities of Europe in the Middle Ages*, repeatedly refers

[1] It appears that Cambridge had precedence in one clause only.
[2] *Parliamentary History of England*, IX, 182. Quoted by Cooper, *op. cit.* III, 309.
[3] Cooper, *op. cit.* III, 486.
[4] Hastings Rashdall, ed. Powicke and Emden, 1936, III, 7, 9, 10.

to the seniority of Oxford, '...A perplexing question', he writes: 'Why should Oxford of all places have become the earliest and greatest national University?' And again: 'Of course, it would be absurd to attempt a demonstration *a priori* that the first and most important English University could have arisen nowhere but at Oxford. But...it will be evident that hardly one other town could be named which satisfied in equal perfection the requirements of the case.' Even this Oxford writer, however, who devotes 273 pages to Oxford and a bare 50 pages to Cambridge, admits 'the obscurity which hangs over the origin of the University'.

Trevelyan,[1] still more recently, accepts the position of Cambridge, as the younger University and agrees that in the fourteenth century thought and education centred in Oxford, but points out that throughout the fifteenth-century Cambridge was gaining ground as a serious rival to Oxford, and that in the Tudor age, 'the younger and hitherto lesser University was coming rapidly to the front, and her sons played a leading part in the great changes of the period'.

Happily, excitement and rivalry have died down, and we can all agree with the writer of a century ago, who said in one of his papers in the *Cambridge Portfolio*: 'The subject was seen to be one in which the real honour or advantage of neither side was at stake; and Cambridge has since been modestly content to take the lower place in the enumeration of the ancient Universities of this land.'

[1] G. M. Trevelyan, *English Social History*, pp. 52, 78, 115.

# CHAPTER VI

# DAMARIS CUDWORTH.—A CAMBRIDGE WOMAN OF THE SEVENTEENTH CENTURY

THERE are few Cambridge women of the long past whose names are remembered, and still fewer of whom we possess any detailed knowledge. It may, therefore, be worth while to recall one who was closely associated with the philosopher, John Locke.

Damaris Cudworth was born in 1658. Her father, Master of Christ's,[1] who had already been Master of Clare Hall, was Regius Professor of Hebrew at Cambridge for forty-three eventful years from 1645 to his death in 1688. Leader of the Cambridge Platonists, Cudworth was, like most of his followers, in political sympathy with the Cromwellians. He was an unusually open-minded controversialist, and takes a high place in the roll of learned English divines; Damaris was therefore brought up in a home in which intellectual independence was valued as well as scholarship.

Dr Cudworth did not marry until he became Master of Christ's in 1654, and Damaris and her brothers were born and brought up in the Master's lodgings in the College. It was at that time customary for the Master of Christ's to let all the chambers that he could spare in his official residence to Noblemen, Fellow Commoners, or

---

[1] There is a portrait of Dr Cudworth in the Hall at Christ's, and his bust stands on a pedestal beside that of Milton at the end of the bathing pool in the Fellows' Garden.

Gentlemen Pensioners, thus increasing the number of students in the college, and also his own income. The larger rooms were reserved for public occasions and for entertaining distinguished guests. Meanwhile, the Master with his family resided in the Master's private lodgings, or the 'Old Lodge', which lay between the College Chapel and Hobson Street. This house, which had been enlarged in 1640, was pulled down in 1748.

There must have been a large family party in the Old Lodge in Dr Cudworth's time, for in addition to his own children, Mrs Cudworth had by a previous marriage a daughter (afterwards Lady Abney) and two sons. Lady Abney married when her step-sister Damaris was only three years old, and then there came into the family circle four grandchildren, all of whom appear in the register of St Andrew-the-Great, at Cambridge, as having been baptized there. There were Cudworth cousins, too, sons of a well-to-do uncle in London, one of whom entered at Christ's in 1677, when fifteen years of age, the usual age of matriculation at that time.

It would be interesting to know more of Damaris Cudworth's childhood in Cambridge. One incident we learn from Dr Covel, her father's successor in the Mastership. He tells how 'in the room where Mr. Maynard keeps'—(Mr Maynard, afterwards Lord Maynard, 'a benefactor of the Physick Garden' kept 'in the Master's over the parlour')—'there was acted (whilst it stood empty) a Pastoral by Dr. Cudworth's Children and some others, contriv'd by Mr. John Andrews afterwards Fellow; To which I myself was courteously admitted as a Spectator.' John Andrews, who contrived the Pastoral, was the eldest step-brother of the Cudworth children.

Dr Covel also mentions in the same unpublished MS.[1] that 'My Lord and Lady Conway and their whole attendance were entertain'd by Dr. Cudworth many dayes, and were lodged partly at his private, and partly in ye publick Lodgings; and they all supped (at a Commencement night) in ye Publick Hall; and several other Persons of Quality have been many times so lodged and entertain'd likewise by him.'

Damaris, as she grew up, became deeply interested in her father's theological and philosophical studies, and was able to take her part in discussion with the learned men, who, in addition to 'Persons of Quality', were entertained at the Lodge. Among these was John Locke. When he first met Damaris Cudworth he was, as she said, 'past the middle age of man, and I but young'—he was a man close on fifty and she but twenty-three. From their first acquaintance they 'conversed freely', and, when a year or two later, Locke retired to Holland in voluntary exile for political reasons, 'he favoured me sometimes with his correspondence', as she modestly put it. Unfortunately, none of the correspondence has been preserved. Locke had, to use his own words in a letter to her brother in India in 1683, already discovered in her a soul 'not of the ordinary alloy'.[2]

While Locke was still drawing out his seven years of exile in Holland, Damaris Cudworth in 1685 married, at the age of twenty-seven, Sir Francis Masham, a widower

---

[1] *Correspondence of Dr Covel*, II, 311. MSS. Add. Mus. Brit, 22, 911. Copied MSS. Univ. Lib. Camb. Quoted by Willis and Clark, *Arch. Hist.* II, 212, 214.

[2] H. R. Fox Bourne, *Life of John Locke*, I, 474.

with nine children, eight sons and a daughter. The following year her only child, Francis Cudworth Masham, was born.

Sir Francis was a grandson of Sir William Masham, who took a conspicuous part on the Parliamentary side in the Civil War and served as a member of Oliver Cromwell's Council. Of the sons of Sir Francis, only the youngest, Samuel, who married Abigail Hill, Queen Anne's favourite, and a few years later became the first Lord Masham, acquired any sort of notoriety.

When political changes made it possible for Locke to return to England, he was frequently with the Mashams at their home at Oates, in Essex. In spite of badly impaired health he was again deeply engaged in public activities, and he found great relief in periodic visits to Oates, where he could enjoy quiet country life in congenial company. So much so, that eventually he was persuaded to make his home there, but he would accept this attractive offer only on condition that Sir Francis Masham would allow him to defray his own expenses. Locke's careful accounts, which have been preserved with part of his library, show his payments to have been at the rate of 20s. per week for himself and his servant, and 1s. per week for a horse at grass. He also records purchases made for Lady Masham, of very diverse nature: 'By two papers of patches, bought in London for my Lady Masham, 1s.' and 'Gassendi's *Astronomica*,[1] for my Lady Masham, 4s. 4d.'

[1] Pierre Gassendi, French philosopher and mathematician (1592–1655). Published *Institutio Astronomica*, 1647; a clear representation of the state of the science in his own day.

When Locke made Oates his permanent home, little Francis was five years of age, 'the only son of a very tender mother', as Locke describes him. The philosopher had developed decided views on the upbringing and education of children, and he and Lady Masham devoted so much time to discussing and applying their theories that Frank must have been in some danger of being subjected to too many experiments. However, taught by his mother (Locke was very firm about this), he made rapid progress, and when he was nine years old, Locke wrote of him that 'he understands Geography and Chronology very well, and the Copernican System of our Vortex; is able to multiply well, and divide a little; and all without ever having one Blow for his Book'.

Physically, the boy became robust under Locke's rule of out-of-door life and exercise, and from being 'almost destroyed by a too tender keeping, he is now by a contrary usage come to bear wind and weather and wet in his Feet,[1] and the Cough which threatened him has left him'. In other ways, also, he must have responded well to the care bestowed upon him, for Locke wrote just before his death, when Francis was nineteen years of age: 'he has never failed to pay me all the respect and do me all the good offices he was capable of performing, with all manner of cheerfulness and delight.'

Life at Oates was full of intellectual interests. Locke had published his great work, *Concerning Human Under-standing*—'the first modern English book'—before he

[1] Locke even went so far as to recommend that a child should 'have his shoes so thin, that they might leak and let in water, whenever he comes near it'. *Thoughts on Education*, ed. 1779, p. 6.

settled at Oates, but he prepared later editions there, and published many other works, including *Some Thoughts on Education*. Lady Masham also produced two small books, *A Discourse Concerning the Love of God*, in which she defends the life of reason against religious theory, and *Thoughts in reference to a Vertuous or Christian Life*, defending a rational life for women against social prejudice. It is not surprising that such a household was but little understood by country neighbours, and Lady Masham may have been describing her own difficulties when she wrote that while, in town, the 'wits' will consider 'as fit to be ridicul'd out of the world' any woman who ordered the 'Course and Manner of her Life something differently from others of her Sex and Condition, in the Country she would probably fare worse'. For, besides other reasons for avoiding her, the neighbourhood will 'already be satisfy'd from the reports of Nurses and Maids that their Lady was indeed a Woman of very odd Whimsies'.

Fortunately, socially as well as intellectually, Lady Masham and her family circle had other resources. They had frequent visitors, including Sir Isaac Newton, Sir Godfrey Kneller, who came twice to paint portraits of Locke and Lady Masham, and many another, until sometimes the house was packed full to overflowing. It may have been Newton who interested Lady Masham in Astronomy and inflicted the Copernican System upon young Francis.

A specially welcome visitor was Peter King, Locke's cousin and, to all intents, his adopted son. Peter, when a boy, was employed in his father's business, but had a voracious appetite for books, and Locke having discovered his ability, persuaded his parents to allow him to study for one of the learned professions. Locke's judgement was justified. Peter King rose successively to be Recorder of London, Lord Chief Justice of the Common Pleas, Lord Chancellor of England, and was ennobled as Lord King of Ockham. His direct descendant in the male line is the Earl of Lovelace. When King was elected to Parliament in 1701, he kept Locke well posted in all that went on, and seems to have been a constant visitor at Oates. Soon after his election, Sir Francis Masham had considerately proposed to Locke that his cousin should 'steal down sometimes with him [Sir Francis] on Saturday, and return on Monday'. At these visits great discussions must have taken place on Currency questions, for Newton was Master of the Mint, with many problems to solve, and Locke had written repeatedly on the subject.

Mrs Cudworth, too, when she left Christ's Lodge after her husband's death in 1688, came to live with her daughter, and the one step-daughter, Esther, remained to brighten the hospitable household and to share in reading aloud to Locke, who was her devoted friend, and whose health, in spite of all the care lavished upon him, continually became worse.

In April 1704 Locke made his Will, leaving the bulk of his personal property to Frank Masham and Peter King, the latter of whom was sole executor and residuary legatee. All his manuscripts were left to King; half his books went to Frank. In the summer, feeling that he could not live long, he earnestly pressed King to come to him, that he might pass some of the last hours of his life 'in the conversation of one who is not only the nearest but the dearest to me of any man in the world'.

Peter King married in September, and Locke rallied sufficiently to give him and his bride a suitable reception at Oates. King was asked to cater for his own wedding-feast at Locke's expense and in accordance with a fine list of dainties drawn up by him. But something, said Locke, might perhaps be omitted in which Mrs King took special delight: 'If there be anything that you can find your wife loves, be sure that provision be made of that, and plentifully, whether I have mentioned it or no.' Well can we picture the pride and pleasure with which the genial old man entertained the wife of his cousin and adopted son—the adopted son whom he had rescued from the grocer's shop at Exeter, and whose future eminence he must now have pretty clearly foreseen. A few days after King left Oates, he solemnly committed to him by letter the care of Frank Masham:

> It is my earnest request to you to take care of the youngest son of Sir Francis and Lady Masham in all his concerns, as if he were your brother. Take care to make him a good, an honest, and an upright man. I have left my directions with him to follow your advice, and I know he will do it; for he never refused to do what I told him was fit.

Peter King certainly executed the dying request of his cousin, so far as Frank Masham's material interests were concerned. Soon after he became Lord Chancellor, Frank Masham was appointed to the newly constituted office of Accountant-General in the Court of Chancery, a lucrative post;[1] later he became one of the Masters in Chancery.

[1] Thomas Fowler, *John Locke*, English Men of Letters, edited by John Morley, pp. 123-5.

The friendship between Locke and Lady Masham ended only with Locke's death in 1704 at the age of seventy-two; the fourteen years he spent at Oates are said to have been the happiest of his life. Lady Masham, writing of him to one of his friends, aptly summed up his character and method of work:

He was always, in the greatest and in the smallest affairs of human life, as well as in speculative opinions, disposed to follow reason, whosoever it were that suggested it; he being ever a faithful servant—I had almost said a slave—to Truth; never abandoning her for anything else, and following her, for her own sake, purely.

Damaris Masham died four years later at Bath, where she rests in the Abbey Church. She was fifty years of age. Locke had written of her some years previously:

The lady is so well versed in theological and philosophical studies, and of such an original mind, that you will not find many men to whom she is not superior in wealth of knowledge and ability to profit by it. Her judgment is excellent, and I know few who can bring such clearness of thought to bear upon the most abstruse subjects, or such capacity for searching through and solving the difficulties of questions beyond the range, I do not say of most women, but even of most learned men.

# CHAPTER VII

# A TOWN PLAN FOR CAMBRIDGE IN THE EIGHTEENTH CENTURY

TOWN-PLANNING in Cambridge is nothing new, nor the need for it. In the British Museum, bound up with a number of old views of the Town, is a manuscript sketch-plan made early in the eighteenth century.[1] This plan was the work of Nicholas Hawksmoor, a pupil of Sir Christopher Wren and later his collaborator.

Hawksmoor was born in 1661, and was therefore twenty-nine years younger than Wren. The first work he is known to have undertaken alone in London was the Church of St Anne's, Limehouse, begun in 1712, one of the fifty churches ordered by an Act of Queen Anne to be built in the Metropolitan area. He must, however, by that time have attained a high reputation in his profession, for he was one of the Commissioners appointed to see that the provisions of Queen Anne's Act were carried through, and he himself was responsible for six of the churches, of which Christ Church in Spitalfields, 1723, the latest of the six, has been described to be as fine a building of its date and kind as can be found in Europe. (Queen Anne's scheme was far too ambitious and it was only found practicable to build eight in all.)

Wren and Hawksmoor both did much work in Oxford, while Wren in his young days had done important work

[1] British Museum, Department of Printed Books (Map Room), *King's Maps and Plans*, VIII, 44.

in Cambridge, beginning in 1663 with Pembroke College Chapel, famous as the first building known to have been carried out by him, undertaken at the behest of his uncle, Matthew Wren, Bishop of Ely. This was followed a few years later by the Chapel and Gallery of Emmanuel College and Trinity College Library. When, in 1690, the woodwork of the Trinity Library was being made and the old Chapel of Pembroke adapted as a library, where Wren's influence appears, he must often have come to Cambridge, and he respected family tradition so far as to send his son to Pembroke as a Fellow Commoner.[1]

Again, in 1698, Sir Christopher and Hawksmoor were engaged in making plans for St John's Third Court and Bridge. Letters from both architects, containing various suggestions, have been preserved and were communicated to the Cambridge Antiquarian Society, in 1891, by Sir R. F. Scott, then Bursar and afterwards Master of the College. Sir Christopher would, therefore, remember Cambridge and its buildings well, when in 1713 Hawksmoor was invited to submit plans for the rebuilding of King's College. The model of his plan for the Fellows' Building, which had obtained Sir Christopher's approval, is still preserved in the College, but ultimately, after much delay, the alternative plan of James Gibbs was adopted. Hawksmoor's sketch-plan for the centre of the Town, with the heading: 'Town of Cambridge as it ought to be reformed', is not dated, but probably originated while he was working at King's.

In order to appreciate Hawksmoor's plan it is necessary

[1] Sir Ellis Minns, in the *Annual Gazette of Pembroke College Cambridge Society*, December 1945.

to imagine King's Parade as it was at that time. The Senate House had not been built, and the site was crowded with taverns and houses, intersected by lanes; hovels (*aediculae*) were actually built up against the walls of Great St Mary's Church—'the west windows are half-blinded up', we read, 'with a Cobbler's and Book-binder's shop' —so that the road was reduced to a width of 25 feet. These unsightly buildings were not removed until 1768.

As there was no Senate House, and the Regent House was too small for ceremonial occasions, the Church itself, which had been the setting for academic 'disputations' in the reign of Elizabeth, was still used for conferring degrees and other ceremonies. It was not convenient for these purposes, and in the opinion of many it was inappropriate that the Church should be put to secular use.[1]

The streets of Cambridge had long been too narrow and congested for the large amount of traffic in and through the town. Thomas Hobson, who died in 1631, thirty years before the birth of Hawksmoor, had been the most famous carrier between Cambridge and London, and was employed by the University as letter-carrier.[2] He had a 'long tilted wayne' on the road, such probably as his father owned before him, described in his will as 'the cart and eight horses, and all the harness and other things thereunto belonging'.[3] By 1661 this type of heavy traffic

[1] See also 'Guildhall and Market Place', Ch. I, p. 11.

[2] The superintendence of the post was reserved to the University in the reign of Anne. As late as 1753, licence was given by the University to eleven persons to carry letters and small parcels. The first mail coach direct to Cambridge from London started to run on 6 February 1792.

[3] Harl. MSS. 6734, quoted in *Cambridge Portfolio*, II, 317.

was becoming a danger to the high ways, and a proclamation was issued forbidding the common practice of
using waggons drawn by eight or ten horses and carrying
sixty to seventy hundredweight.

In Hobson's time, personal travel was undertaken on
horseback (his own figure on his horse is well known) or
by family coach; it was not until 1653 that the first public
passenger coach took the road from Cambridge. It started
from a post-house, the Devil's Tavern, one of the taverns
on the present site of the Senate House.

From that time onwards with the gradual improvement
of the roads there was clearly a steady increase in means
of transport, for a Cambridge Guide of 1763 gives 'An
Exact List of the Posts, Coaches, Stage-Waggons and other
Carriers' plying between Cambridge and London, Norwich, Bury, Huntingdon, Stamford, Ipswich, Yarmouth,
Colchester, Kettering, Leicester, Birmingham and Coventry, Lynn and Wisbech—the list occupying more than two
pages of small print in Cooper's *Annals of Cambridge*.[1]

It may be assumed, therefore, that by 1713, when
Hawksmoor was in Cambridge, many coaches, bearing
such names as the 'Telegraph', the 'Union', the 'Fly',[2]
the 'Rising Sun', and the 'Patriot', were helping to create
traffic problems. The 'Telegraph' coach was celebrated
in a ballad of thirty-five verses, written by Henry Thomp-
son of St John's,[3] who in 1820 missed the Chancellor's
Gold medal for an English poem but received an extra

---

[1] Cooper, IV, 115–16.
[2] Gunning, in his *Reminiscences*, 1798, mentions the coach 'so well
known by the name of the Fly', II, 116.
[3] J. J. Smith, *Cambridge Portfolio*, II, 457.

prize. The ballad describes the experiences of a reckless driver of the 'Telegraph', who flouted the Devil, with disastrous results. It may have been suggested by the fact that the first passenger coach started from the Devil's Tavern.

The last stage coach plied between Cambridge and London in October 1845. To celebrate the centenary of its disappearance, the *Cambridge Daily News* reprinted the following paragraph from its predecessor, the *Cambridge Chronicle*, for the week ended 1 November 1845:

We have seen the last of those elegant conveyances, the London coaches, upon which Cambridge used to look with pride. Last Saturday the 'Beehive' ran its last stage; the contest against all-potent steam was found to be useless, and the reins were given up after a struggle of a few months. We are glad to record that the victor has been at least merciful, for Wilkins, the civil driver of the 'Beehive', has been provided for by a berth upon the rail.

The Railway Station at Cambridge had been opened on 30 July 1845.

To complete the picture of the centre of the Town, it must be remembered that houses surrounded the south and east sides of St Mary's, sometimes known as St Mary-by-the-Market, and that the space on Market Hill was further restricted by a large block of shops and houses; another group, standing at the back of St Edward's Church, narrowed the approach to Peas Hill. The old Town Hall and Gaol occupied part of the site of the present Guildhall, another part was covered with open booths for market purposes.

( 131 )    9-2

Such were the conditions when Nicholas Hawksmoor made his plan for reforming Cambridge.

Starting from the Great Bridge in Magdalene Street, then of timber and in bad condition, which Hawksmoor would have rebuilt and widened, he planned to widen also the two main thoroughfares through the Town. There would have been a set-back in Bridge Street, Sidney Street and St Andrew's Street, providing a wide and direct road to 'Hogmagog'.

As the Senate House did not yet exist and the Water-house Building of Caius College was in the far future, it seemed comparatively easy to provide a fine sweep of road from Trumpington Street through Trinity Street to a widened St John's Street, the only serious obstruction being the Church of All Saints, which then projected over the pathway opposite St John's College, and was not removed to Jesus Lane until 1865.

Petty Cury,[1] then as now, presented a difficult problem, intensified at that time by the existence of several coaching inns. Hawksmoor, nothing daunted, bravely said: 'Petty Cury, *ampliat*', and amplified it was to be, by making a new line from about the middle of the north side east-wards, gradually widening the road and cutting off a large corner at the junction with Sidney Street. The open space thus visualized was not provided until more than 200 years later, while the Cury itself still remains 'unamplified'.

---

[1] 'It is not improbable that part of the Market Hill was anciently called the Cury or Cooks' Row and that the street which is at a right angle with the Market Hill was called the *Petty* Cury to distinguish it from the other or greater Cury.' *Proceedings of C.A.S.* i, 63.

## Town Plan for Cambridge

Hawksmoor further proposed a covered market—'Forum', he called it—between Great St Mary's and St Edward's Passage. The former Church he would have given over to the Corporation, while St Edward's was to disappear, and a new University Church, together with the Senate House, were to stand side by side linked by a fine archway on King's Parade opposite King's College.

The scheme was an ambitious one, and Hawksmoor knew it. On a corner of the map, in his own handwriting and signed in his own name, appears the following apology: 'It would be very impertinent in me to desire so much good and I humbly ask pardon for making such a plan, and hope I may be excused because Cavalier Fontaine and others have done the same in cases of like nature.'

This inscription is typical of Hawksmoor, who was essentially a modest man. Mr Goodhart-Rendel, writing of him in the Masters of Architecture Series, says that the best clue to his character which we possess is Vanbrugh's often quoted request to the Duke of Marlborough 'for some opportunity to do him good, because he does not seem very solicitous to do it for himself'.[1] The same writer complains that

fame deals partially with artists, robbing one to enrich another, bestowing and conferring favours according to her whim. Towards Nicholas Hawksmoor, architect, she has been especially unkind, ascribing much of his produce to other authorship and making little of the rest. Thus has she kept in the second rank a reputation which, had she chosen, might have equalled that of any of her favourites. If a building of

[1] E. S. Goodhart-Rendel, *Nicholas Hawksmoor*, p. 18.

Hawksmoor's please, fame credits it to Wren: if it fail to please, then Hawksmoor can have it.[1]

It must be remembered that under Wren he was in charge of the works at Kensington Palace, and at the Hospitals of Greenwich and Chelsea, while with Sir John Vanbrugh he supervised the work on Blenheim Palace and Castle Howard.

Failure to give him all the credit that he deserved was no doubt due to his humility. It is interesting to find that it was for Cambridge that he proposed one of his boldest schemes, and if his dream had materialized, he would have done for Cambridge something of what his master, Christopher Wren, had dreamt of doing for London.

[1] Goodhart-Rendel, *op. cit.* p. 7.

# CHAPTER VIII

# MENDICITY HOUSE

## SIDELIGHTS ON SOCIAL CONDITIONS IN CAMBRIDGE IN THE NINETEENTH CENTURY

MENDICITY HOUSE was an important feature of two successive social experiments undertaken in Cambridge in the nineteenth century, the earlier of which, the Anti-Mendicity Society, was the direct forerunner of the present Central Aid Society.

Following the Napoleonic Wars, widespread distress, due to lack of employment and the high price of food, resulted in the appearance of a drifting population in search of work or precarious maintenance by the charity of the public. The London Mendicity Society was founded in 1818 to deal with the problem. Cambridge, also suffering from an influx of these unfortunate persons, who, reduced to vagrancy and beggary, beset the Backs of the Colleges in particular, followed the example of London in 1819.

At a meeting of the Vice-Chancellor and other members of the University, and of the Magistrates and principal inhabitants of the Town of Cambridge, held on 8 May 1819, at Magdalene College, for the purpose of considering the propriety of establishing a Society for the Suppression of Mendicity, it was resolved unanimously:

1. That the Precincts of the University and the Town of Cambridge have long been much infested with Beggars and Vagrants.

2. That this class of persons, besides obtaining alms upon false pretences, are often guilty of extorting money by threats, of stealing in College rooms and dwelling-houses, and of committing various depredations in the vicinity of the Town, and that they not infrequently bring along with them fevers, small-pox, and other infectious diseases.

3. That it is expedient to establish a Society for the suppression of Vagrancy and Mendicity, within the limits of the Town and University, by furthering the execution of the laws made for that purpose, and by discouraging the practice of giving money to beggars.

4. That an active and intelligent person be employed by the Society at a Salary hereafter to be agreed upon, who shall make it his whole business to look out for, and with the assistance of the Constables, to apprehend and carry before a Magistrate all vagrants who shall be found begging in our streets, walks and highways, and also all petty chapmen and pedlars, who are not duly licensed, or otherwise authorised by law; and to write a description of every person so apprehended in a book to be kept for that purpose.

5. That the Magistrates of the Town and County, present at this Meeting, are determined to proceed to conviction against, and to punish with the utmost severity of the law, all such delinquents and all who are convicted of lodging and harbouring them, contrary to the Statute.

Further resolutions were passed with regard to action that could be recommended within the Colleges, including a request that Tutors of Colleges should point out to their pupils the impropriety of giving money to beggars.

The document embodying these resolutions was signed by George Neville, Vice-Chancellor, Charles Musgrave, James Burleigh, John Purchas, Thomas Mortlock, Charles Finch, and twenty others.

## Mendicity House

No record has been found of the actual duration of this vigorous method of repression, but it is clear that the Society lapsed before 1838, for the Report of the Charity Commissioners in that year states, in reference to Hobson's Workhouse (or the Spinning House), that it was 'used for the reception of persons sent by the Mendicity Society of Cambridge *so long as it existed*; & vagrants not belonging to the town or university were sent there, relieved & discharged'.

A new Society which adopted the same name took its rise at a public Meeting held in the Town Hall on 18 March 1847. The purely repressive attitude with regard to vagrants and beggars adopted by the original Society had been abandoned, and the object now was to assist artisans or labourers journeying in search of work by supplying them with a meal and shelter for the night.

Mendicity House now comes into the picture. In February 1848 a portion of what was described as the Old Manor House in Barnwell was opened by the recently formed Anti-Mendicity Society for the reception of needy travellers under the charge of a resident Constable and Matron. After it had been in use for six years, 1848–54, it was stated that upwards of 12,000 travellers had been relieved, an average of about forty a week. From its connexion with the Society this house, of which the earlier history has been lost, came to be known as Mendicity House, and thirty years later, when the property had to be sold, the surrounding houses and the back-land were grouped with the large house under the name of the Mendicity Property.

For more than twenty years the new Committee carried

on the work on the lines laid down in 1847, serving a useful, but very limited, purpose. And then, fifty-two years after the Society's original formation, a breath of fresh life came into its Committee room, for in the spring of 1871, Henry Sidgwick of Trinity College, feeling the need of 'doing some practically useful work'—to use the words of his biographers—joined the Committee and became an active member. After sharing in the work for eight years, he formed the opinion that a fundamental change must be made if the Society was to do really effective work for the community, and in 1879 he actually induced the Society to dissolve itself, preparatory to re-organization on the lines of the recently formed London Charity Organization Society. A few months later, the same Committee, with a new Constitution and strengthened by new adherents, emerged as the Cambridge Charity Organization Society, but preserving the old name of Anti-Mendicity Society as a sub-title until the year 1894. The same course was followed when, in 1915, in order to impress upon the public the constructive side of the Society's work, the additional title of 'Central Aid' was adopted (although without any change in the Constitution), and the sub-title of Charity Organization Society was continued until 1919. The essential continuity of the work has thus been clearly marked.

The last report of the Anti-Mendicity Society, given by the Secretary in 1879, calls attention, not to its disappearance, but to an important extension of its sphere of work:

It is proposed to extend the operations of the Mendicity Society so as to enable the inhabitants of Cambridge to extend their sympathies to the really deserving poor without increasing the intolerable evil of the tramp system, and the mendicity and mendacity of those resident beggars who prey upon the generous and well-to-do.

There was nothing premature or hurried in this decision to take a step forward. Henry Sidgwick had done his best on the old lines for eight years. As one of his friends wrote of him after his death: 'Those who came to Henry Sidgwick for practical advice knew that he would omit nothing from his view, and understand all, and that his decision would be founded in justice and charity.' Another friend wrote: 'He was prompt and decided when immediate action was necessary, though his insight into consequences often induced caution where less thoughtful persons would have hurried on more rapidly.'

A leaflet issued to explain to subscribers and the public generally the change in the attitude of the Society bears the impress of Sidgwick. It contained the following passages:

The Committee of the Mendicity Society desire to call the attention of the inhabitants of Cambridge to the important extension of work that has recently taken place. Hitherto it has been thought best to confine its operations to wayfarers. But no conviction has more deeply and universally impressed itself upon all who have studied the difficult problem of pauperism, than that all almsgiving without examination aggravates the evil which it is intended to palliate. At the same time it is impossible, even if it were desirable, to check the casual charity of sympathetic persons without providing them with some substitute; rather than neglect real distress, they will relieve the counterfeit. The only remedy is to arrange for the distribution of alms through the agency of practised almoners. Wayfarers will still be fed and lodged as before [but in recognized lodging-houses, no longer in the Society's hostel]; residents, who are ascertained to be really deserving of relief, will either obtain it from the Society's funds, or be referred to some one of the existing charitable organisations. This scheme requires the widest possible co-operation on the part of the public; as the efficiency of the organisation will increase in proportion as it is generally used.

On these foundations, well and truly laid, the Society has built up its work. With changes in the social outlook, the structure has from time to time been reconditioned and enlarged, new vistas have been opened up, much pioneer and experimental work has been undertaken, anticipating by many years ultimate action by the State or the local authority, thus illustrating in striking fashion the traditional English method of trying out new forms of social service before making them statutory.

But this subsequent history must be left untold, while we follow the fortunes of Mendicity House.

In 1847, when the tenancy of the Old Manor House was acquired by the Anti-Mendicity Society, it was in the ownership of Thomas Parker, Broker, of Cambridge, who left it with other property to his wife for her life. She died in 1856 and, her son having predeceased her, the property had to be divided among his nine children. By successive Indentures over the period 1865 to 1872, the surviving sons and daughters conveyed all their grandfather's estate to their youngest brother, Octavius Parker, a well-known local auctioneer.

Octavius evidently undertook responsibilities which he was unable to meet, for after his death in 1876, an Order of the High Court of Justice, Chancery Division, was made directing that all his property should be sold for the benefit of his creditors. It was probably at this point that the Anti-Mendicity Society gave up their tenancy.

The sale of this property, which was advertised to take place in August 1878, led to the second social experiment in which Mendicity House played a part.

When it became known that, in addition to the Mendicity property, a considerable amount of poor cottage property belonging to the same owner would be included in the sale, a number of public spirited members of the Town and University, who were distressed by the bad housing conditions in Barnwell, got together with commendable rapidity and took preliminary steps to form the Cambridge Improved Industrial Dwellings Co. Ltd. with the object of acquiring and improving cottage property as opportunity offered.

When the sale took place in August 1878, there had not been time for the necessary formalities, and the Association was not incorporated until a fortnight later. So great was the zeal of the pioneers, however, that on behalf of a company not yet formed and with cash not the half of which had been subscribed, almost the whole of the property put up for sale was bought at a cost of £3472. In order to meet the deficit £1064 was advanced by three members and an overdraft of £1035 obtained from the Bank.

The prospectus of the Company shows that it was a true pioneer of schemes later undertaken by the State and local authorities. It ran as follows:

This Company has been formed for the purpose of providing healthy and comfortable dwellings, the acquiring of land and dwellings, the building of dwellings, and the selling and disposing of such land and dwellings, either absolutely or leasing the same on terms for converting the occupancy into ownership by means of purchase instalments, and the providing, letting, maintaining and regulating of buildings with fittings and conveniences for the benefit of the Company's tenants and others.

The deplorable condition of some of the houses in Barnwell has for a long time engaged the anxious attention of philanthropic persons in Cambridge. The Medical Officer of Health has more than once animadverted on the unwholesome state of some of the courts; and some buildings have recently been condemned by the Sanitary Authority as unfit for human habitation. Dwellings of this kind tend to the moral degradation of their occupants, and lower the whole tone of their neighbourhood. The announcement of the sale by public auction on the 28th day of August last of a considerable amount of the lowest class of house property, suggested to several gentlemen that the best way to meet the case would be to organize a Company for the purpose of buying this and other property of the kind, as it should come into the market, with a view to improve or rebuild it, and open, where practicable, thoroughfares through the blind alleys.

The Company affords an opportunity of doing much good in Cambridge. Decent tenements will draw decent tenants who will leaven the neighbourhood in which they dwell; and on all their own property the Company will be able to impose rules which will tend to the cleanliness and health of the inhabitants and thereby help them to a higher social and moral level.

It is the wish of the promoters to engage the interest of as many as possible of the Members of the University and of their fellow Townsmen in this undertaking.

Among the first subscribers who took up shares were men whose names are still familiar in Cambridge: Professor

## Mendicity House

Adams, William Bond, John Burford, R. C. Burrows, H. J. Church, C. J. Clay, John Death, John Ellison, George Foster, Rev. A. E. Humphreys, Professor Liveing, J. Odell Pain, James Sanders, Robert Sayle, Rev. C. E. Searle, John Webb, Mark Ives Whibley, and S. L. Young.

It is probable that the initiative came from Mr Humphreys, Vicar of St Matthew's, who was greatly concerned about the condition of housing in his parish. It was he who persuaded Dr Sidgwick to buy twenty houses in Vicarage Terrace, which Mrs Sidgwick, before leaving Cambridge, presented to the Central Aid Society.[1]

When the Company had thus been formed, work on the property proceeded vigorously, and at the end of nine months, the Directors reported that fifteen dilapidated tenements had been demolished, twenty-five more cleansed and repaired, and the erection of twenty-five improved dwellings begun. After enlarging upon the improvements that had been effected, the Directors claimed that 'a veritable moral and social besom of reformation' had been applied, and the whole aspect of the district round St Matthew's Church had been so changed for the better, that the Directors hoped it would commend itself to the favourable judgement of the community.

In the course of the same year, a tender of £920 was accepted for building improved dwellings on a site at the corner of Crispin Street and East Road. Two of the houses were taken over by the Rev. H. Trotter and Mr C. J. Clay for opening a Coffee Tavern and Lodging House. These, with a third added later, and all three thrown into one,

[1] Half of these houses were destroyed and several lives lost in the first bombing attack on Cambridge in 1940.

were at first managed by the Barnwell Coffee House Committee, and subsequently for many years by the British Women's Temperance Association, under the name of the White Ribbon. The building later became the White Ribbon Temperance Hotel, under the management of the Salvation Army.

Not content with all these activities, a tender of £1185 was accepted for building eleven cottages on the garden behind Mendicity House, the road being named Leeke Street, after a former vicar of the parish.

The next few years were mainly occupied in carrying out minor improvements and working off the adverse Bank balance, until in 1884 ground was acquired in Castle End, and eighteen cottages were erected in Gloucester Street. These were designed towards meeting the needs of a large class, who could not afford to pay more than half-a-crown a week, and as much accommodation was given as could be provided for the money. Needless to say, they were all let.

In 1888 the Directors reported a considerable loss by reduced rents and empty houses in St Matthew's parish, mainly due to the rapid development of Romsey Town, which depreciated older cottage property on that side of Cambridge. Attention was accordingly turned to other parts of the town, and in 1890 houses were again built in Castle End.

Interest was paid usually at the rate of 4 per cent, income tax free, but by 1923 the gross rentals having amounted to £1351, in that year and the following, 5 per cent interest was paid.

Professor Liveing had been Chairman from the foundation of the Company in 1878 until his retirement in 1923 at the age of ninety-six.

By that time the Company had lost its impetus, and the Directors reported that 'taking into consideration the altered conditions of the Housing question, they deemed it desirable that the holdings should be realized at the best possible prices obtainable. The return of capital to shareholders is expected to amount to about £3. 10. 0 per £5 share.'

Thus ended an early experiment in housing, which, although it had not realized all the hopes with which its founders set out, yet played a useful part in the life of the community during its run of almost half a century.

# APPENDIX

## 'CAMBRIDGE' AS A PLACE-NAME IN OTHER PARTS OF THE WORLD

*U.S.A.:*     There is a 'Cambridge' in each of the following States:

| | |
|---|---|
| Idaho | Missouri |
| Illinois | Nebraska |
| Iowa | New Hampshire |
| Kansas | New York |
| Maine | Ohio |
| Maryland | Pennsylvania |
| Massachusetts | S. Carolina |
| Michigan | Vermont |
| Minnesota | Wisconsin |

There are also:

Cambridge City, Indiana.
Cambridgeport, Vermont.
Cambridge Springs, Pennsylvania.

*Canada:*     Cambridge, Ontario.
Cambridge, Nova Scotia.
Cambridge, New Brunswick.
Cambridge Bay, N.W. Territories.

## Appendix

| | |
|---|---|
| *Australia:* | Cambridge Gulf, W. Australia. |
| | Cambridge Downs, Queensland. |
| | Cambridge, Tasmania. |
| *New Zealand:* | Cambridge, Auckland. |
| *South Africa:* | Cambridge, Cape Province. |
| *West Indies:* | Cambridge, Jamaica. |
| *South America:* | Cambridge Island, Chile. |
| *Arctic:* | Cambridge Bay, Alexandra Land. |

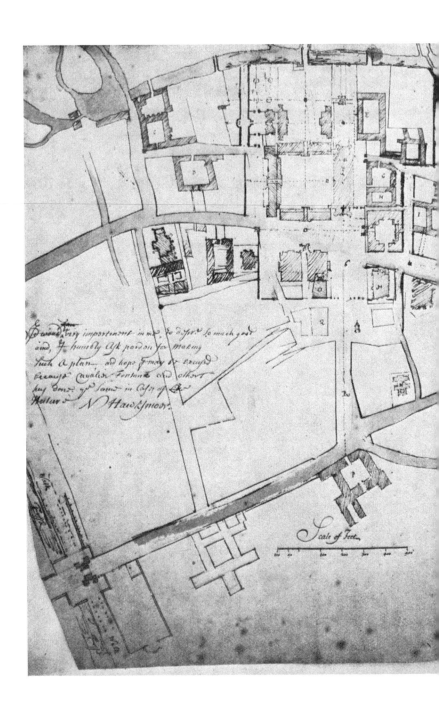

I would ... very impertinent in me ... so ... so much good and, I humbly Ask pardon for making Such a plan, and hope I may be excused because Cavalier Fontana and others have done y.e Same in Cases of ... Nature.

N. Hawksmoor.

Scale of Feet.

Plate XIV. Hawksmoor's Plan for Cambridge (*c.* 1713)

# INDEX OF NAMES

# Index of Names

# Index of Names

# Index of Names

# Index of Names

Hacket, John, Bishop, 78, 80
Harding, Colonel T.W., 54
Hardwicke, Lord Chancellor, 82
Harley, Robert, first Earl of Oxford, 82
Harley, Edward, second Earl of Oxford, 50, 81, 82
Harrison, Jane, xii
Harvey Road, xviii, xix
Harvey, William, xviii
Haslingfield, 104, 111
Hastings, 59
Hatcher, Dr John, 10, 11, 12, 72
Hatcher, Sir John, 12
Hatfield Peverel, 84
Haviland, Dr, 107
Hawkins, Sir John, 78
Hawkins, Sir Richard, 66
Hawksmoor, Sir Nicholas, xxiv, 127 ff.
Henrietta Maria, 78
Henry I, 58, 84, 115
Henry III, 3, 26, 58, 93
Henry VI, 64
Henry VII, 64, 67
Henry VIII, 65, 104
Herb Market, 6
Hereford, 37
Hertford, 37
Higden, Ranulf, 97
Hill, Abigail, the Lady Masham, 121
Hills Road, xvii, xviii, xxi
Hobson's Conduit, 5, 47
Hobson's Spinning House or Work-house, xvii, 137
Hobson Street, 119
Hobson, Thomas, 5 n., 129, 130
Hock Tuesday, 33
Hogmagog, see Gogmagog
Holles, John, Duke of Newcastle, 82

Holy Trinity Church, 73, 75, 77
Holy Trinity Parish, 72
Honey Hill, 2
Horseheath Hall, 50
Howard, John, 14
Howard, Thomas, third Duke of Norfolk, 38, 39
Howard, Thomas, fourth Duke of Norfolk, 34, 39
Howard, Henry FitzAlan, fifteenth Duke of Norfolk, xvii
Hugh, Bishop of Ely, 90
Hull, 62
Humphreys, Rev. A. E., 143
Huntingdon, 84, 91, 130
Hurrell, Swann, Mayor of Cambridge, 53
Hyde, Edward, Earl of Clarendon, 44, 45, 46
Hyde, Sir Nicholas, Chief Justice, 45
Hythe, 59

Ingulph, Abbot of Croyland, 109
Ipswich, 37, 66, 130
Isabella of France, 90
Isle of Ely, see Ely

James I, 42
James II, 8, 48
Jermyn, Henry, Lord Dover, 48
Joan of Arc, 60
Jesus Lane, 132
John of Malvern, 97, 98
John, King, 90
Jolan de Thorleye, Prior of Barnwell, 92, 93, 107

Kensington Palace, 134
Kerrich, Rev. Thomas, 19
Kettering, 130

# Index of Names

# Index of Names

# Index of Names

# Index of Names

## Index of Names

Printed in the United Kingdom by
Lightning Source UK Ltd., Milton Keynes
141865UK00001B/9/P